SELECTED CHAPTERS FROM

DAVISON: ABNORMAL PSYCHOLOGY, 3rd CANADIAN EDITION

A Wiley Canada Custom Publication
for

Trent University

PSYC240

Wiley Canada Custom Services
JOHN WILEY & SONS CANADA, LTD.

Cover Photo Credit: Jason Vandenberg

Printed and bound in the United States
10 9 8 7 6 5 4 3 2 1

John Wiley & Sons Canada, Ltd
6045 Freemont Blvd.
Mississauga, Ontario
L5R 4J3
Visit our website at: www.wiley.ca

THIRD CANADIAN EDITION

abnormal
PSYCHOLOGY

GERALD C. DAVISON
University of Southern California

KIRK R. BLANKSTEIN
University of Toronto

GORDON L. FLETT
York University

JOHN M. NEALE
State University of New York at Stony Brook

John Wiley & Sons Canada, Ltd.

Library and Archives Canada Cataloguing in Publication

Abnormal psychology/Gerald C. Davison ...[et al.]. –3rd Canadian ed

ISBN 978-0-470-84072-6

1. Psychology, Pathological –Textbooks. I. Davison, Gerald C.
RC454.A255 2007   616.89
C2007-905395-5

Author Photo Credits
v: Photo of Gerald Davison courtesy Irene Fertik
v: Photo of Kirk Blankstein courtesy Gord Flett
v: Photo of Gordon Flett courtesy Glen Flett
vi: Photo of John Neale courtesy John Neale

Production Credits
Publisher: Veronica Visentin
Acquisitions Editor: Michael Valerio
Editorial Manager: Karen Staudinger
Vice President, Publishing Services: Karen Bryan
Publishing Services Manager: Ian Koo
Marketing Manager: Joan Lewis-Milne
New Media Editor: Elsa Passera
Developmental Editor: Zoë Craig
Cover & Design: Jason Vandenberg
Typesetting: Prepare

Printing & Binding: Quebecor World Inc.
Cover Image: Marian Dale Scott, Canadian 1906–1993, Escalator 1936, Oil on board
© Estate of Marian Dale Scott, c/o Christopher Varley, Toronto, ON.
Printed and bound in United States of America

12 11 10 09 08 QW 5 4 3 2 1

John Wiley & Sons Canada, Ltd.

John Wiley & Sons Canada, Ltd.
6045 Freemont Blvd.
Mississauga, Ontario L5R 4J3
Visit our website at: www.wiley.ca

LEGAL AND ETHICAL ISSUES

"The myth is that if people exhibit bizarre behaviour, men in white coats will come and take you away. There aren't any people who can do that. If only there were."
—Fay Herrick, a Calgarian whose son suffers from schizophrenia (Nichols, 1995.)

"The idea that patients would heal faster within their communities is bizarre. These same patients originally came from the communities whose healing qualities clearly were not sufficient to prevent them from becoming sick in the first place. The notion that patients would heal faster in the bosom of their families is equally problematic. Many families are too sick, or too tired, or simply do not have the resources or the energy to cope with very sick patients."
—Abram Hoffer, former director of psychiatric research for the Province of Saskatchewan, currently in private practice in Victoria, B.C. and president of the Canadian Schizophrenia Foundation (2000. p. 145)

"CTOs [community treatment orders] may very well be an expression of both the best and the worst in current psychiatric practice. At best, we are looking at paternalism—benevolent coercion respectful of autonomy and liberty. At worst, we ignore the concerns of fairness and justice. . . . Just exactly how do we balance autonomy and paternalism?
—Gary A. Chaimowitz, from a guest editorial in the **Canadian Journal of Psychiatry** (2004, p. 578)

George Agnew Reid, 1860–1947, *The Other Side of the Question,* 1890 oil on canvas, 104.0 × 132.5 cm, Art Gallery of Ontario, Toronto Purchase, 1985.

©2007 AGO

SECTION 1—Guarantee of Rights and Freedoms. The Canadian Charter of Rights and Freedoms guarantees the rights and freedoms set out in it subject only to such reasonable limits prescribed by law as can be demonstrably justified in a free and democratic society.

Section 2—Fundamental Freedoms. Everyone has the following fundamental freedoms: 1. freedom of conscience and religion; 2. freedom of thought, belief, opinion and expression; including freedom of the press and other media of communication; 3. freedom of peaceful assembly; and 4. freedom of association.

Section 7—Legal Rights. Everyone has the right to life, liberty and security of the person and the right not to be deprived thereof except in accordance with the principles of fundamental justice.

Section 8—Everyone has the right to be secure against unreasonable search or seizure.

Section 9—Everyone has the right not to be arbitrarily detained or imprisoned.

Section 12—Everyone has the right not to be subjected to any cruel and unusual treatment or punishment.

Section 15—Equality before and under law and equal protection and benefit of law. Every individual is equal before and under the law and has the right to equal protection and benefits of the law without discrimination, and, in particular, without discrimination based on race, national, or ethnic origin, colour, religion, sex, age or mental or physical disability.

We open our final chapter in this way, with sections of the *Canadian Charter of Rights and Freedoms* (1982), for two reasons. First, the legal and mental health systems collaborate continually, although often subtly, to deny a substantial proportion of the Canadian population their basic civil rights. With the best of intentions, judges, tribunals, governing boards of hospitals, bar associations, and professional mental health groups have worked over the years to protect society at large from the actions of people regarded as mentally ill or mentally disordered and considered dangerous to themselves or to others. However, in so doing, they have denied many thousands of people their basic civil rights.

Second, Section 15 (1) of the *Charter of Rights and Freedoms* (i.e., Equality before and under law) is especially significant because it extends the right of equality to mentally ill people. According to Eaves, Lamb, and Tien (2000), Canada "is one of the few countries in the world that explicitly extends the general rights found in our constitution to people who are mentally ill" (p. 615). It is up to each province to formulate and implement laws that are in keeping with the Charter of Rights and Freedoms. Although all provinces share the same Charter-driven principles in their legislation, differences exist in how these principles are realized. Another possible source of differences between the provinces is the "notwithstanding clause," which permits provinces to opt out of the Charter if they perceive a conflict between their goals and values and the overall goals and values of the nation.

Although mentally ill people are extended rights under the equality provision, there are situations in which other principles come into effect. Specifically, the *Charter of Rights and Freedoms* also includes provisions that allow for some people to be removed from society if they act in a way that infringes on the rights of other people to a free and democratic society. In other words, at times, the needs of the society as a whole may outweigh the needs of any one individual. Mentally ill individuals who have broken the law, or who are alleged to have done so, may be subject to a loss of liberty where their mental disorder becomes relevant to the criminal prosecution because of either concerns regarding fitness to stand trial or criminal responsibility. In other words, they may be subject to criminal commitment, a procedure that may confine a person in a mental institution either for determination of competency to stand trial or after a verdict of not criminally responsible on account of mental disorder. Part XX.1 of the *Criminal Code of Canada* provides a "mini-code" that sets out the procedures for dealing with mentally disordered individuals who find themselves before the criminal courts. Civil commitment, provided for in provincial statutes, is a procedure by which a mentally ill and dangerous person who may not have broken a law can be deprived of liberty and incarcerated in a psychiatric hospital. Both committal procedures—one federal, the other provincial—may result in a loss of liberty as a result of mental disorder. In this chapter, we look at these legal procedures in depth. We then turn to an examination of some important ethical issues as they relate to therapy and research.

CRIMINAL COMMITMENT

Historically, much of Canadian law has derived from English common law, reflecting the British influence in Canada. The exception is Quebec, where Napoleonic law has been incorporated into civil statutes. In Canada, criminal law is a matter of federal statute and is therefore the same in every province. Matters of health law, however, are determined at a provincial level and can differ from province to province. Our criminal code was first enacted in 1892, when we adopted a "draft" British code that was never enacted in Britain. Britain, to this day, has no criminal code. Almost as early as the concept of *mens rea*, or "guilty mind," and the rule "No crime without an evil intent" had begun to be accepted in English common law, "insanity" had to be taken into consideration, for a disordered mind may be regarded as unable to formulate and carry out a criminal purpose (Morse, 1992). In other words, a disordered mind cannot be a guilty mind; only a guilty mind can engender culpable actions.

Initially, insanity was not a trial defence, but in England, the Crown sometimes granted pardons to people who had been convicted of homicide if they were judged completely and totally "mad" (Morris, 1968). By the reign of Edward I (1272–1307), the concept of insanity had begun to be argued in court and could lessen punishment. It became the rule of law during the course of the fourteenth century that a person proved to be wholly and continually mad could be defended against a criminal charge.

In today's courts, judges and lawyers call on psychiatrists and clinical psychologists for assistance in dealing with criminal acts thought to result from the accused person's disordered mental state rather than from free will. Are such emotionally disturbed perpetrators less criminally responsible than those who are not distraught but commit the same crimes? Should such individuals even be brought to trial for transgressions against society's laws? Although efforts to excuse or protect an accused person by invoking the insanity defence or by judging him or her unfit to stand trial are undoubtedly well intentioned, invoking these doctrines can often subject those accused to a greater denial of liberty than they would otherwise experience.

THE NOT CRIMINALLY RESPONSIBLE DEFENCE

IN HAMILTON, Lucia Piovesan had been diagnosed as having had paranoid schizophrenia for over 20 years, but she received minimal treatment because she did not take her antipsychotic drugs. Moreover, she resisted family requests to get additional treatment. Her neighbours, Tony Antidormi and his wife, Lori Triano-Antidormi (a former graduate student in psychology at York University), tried unsuccessfully on several occasions to convince police that Piovesan was dangerous. In March 1997, Piovesan stabbed to death the Antidormis' 2-year-old son, Zachery, after becoming convinced that he was the soul of her dead son and was asking for release (see Prete, 2000). Piovesan was found not criminally responsible because of her paranoid schizophrenia.

Dorothy Joudrie, a wealthy Calgary socialite, apparently endured years of abuse from her former husband, Earl Joudrie, and as a result, developed a problem with alcoholism. The situation escalated in January 1995 when Joudrie shot her former husband six times and was arrested for attempted murder. Her lawyer argued that, at the time of the crime, Joudrie was in a dissociative, trance-like state (a condition known as automatism) and had no recollection of her actions. In May 1996, a jury found her not criminally responsible owing to a mental disorder, and she was confined at the Alberta Hospital in Edmonton for five months. Joudrie's mental state improved greatly over time, and she received an absolute discharge on October 20, 1998 (Martin, 1998). Until her death in 2002, she acted as an advocate for the rights of mentally ill people.

On May 28, 1998, two teenagers from British Columbia were killed when struck by a car driven by Julia Campagna of Seattle, Washington. Campagna's car was speeding and smashed into the back of the teenagers' car at the Canadian Customs border crossing. The driver was charged with dangerous driving causing death, but on September 3, 1999, a B.C. court ruled that Campagna was not criminally responsible on account of mental disorder. The accident occurred while Campagna was in a psychotic state. She had symptoms of psychosis after taking the diet drug Xenadrine to lose weight for a marathon running race. Campagna thought that she was in an airplane rather than a car and that she was hearing the voice of Canadian NHL hockey player Joe Nieuwendyk on her radio. She was following the voice's instructions, believing she was on her way to a rendezvous with Nieuwendyk to conceive a child with him.

Because her symptoms were deemed to be due to the pills she was taking (a finding that was confirmed by a B.C. Children's Commission investigation [see McLintock, 2001]), Campagna was released and allowed to go free, having been found not criminally responsible. The court ruled that Campagna posed no risk to the public and could not be held. Julie Campagna subsequently launched a civil lawsuit against the drug manufacturer and other parties, and the families of the deceased launched civil lawsuits against Campagna and the drug manufacturer (see the Canadian Press, 2000).

The three cases described above all involved high-profile situations in which defendants in Canadian courts were found not criminally responsible for their acts on account of mental disorder (NCRMD). The so-called insanity defence, NCRMD involves the legal argument that a defendant should not be held responsible for an otherwise illegal act if it is attributable to mental illness that interferes with rationality or that results in some other excusing circumstance, such as not knowing right from wrong. Mental disorder may operate to negate the requisite mental element (*mens rea*), or it may operate to render the act (*actus reus*) involuntary. Or, it may operate to provide a supervening defence even where the requisite mental element and act have been proven. For example, an accused may specifically intend to kill his neighbour, believing him to be an alien sent to destroy the world. Here, the court may find that, notwithstanding the requisite elements having been proven, the accused did not appreciate the nature and consequences of his act or know it to be wrong. A staggering amount of material has been written on this defence, and public outcries continue to emerge in prominent cases in which the defendant is found not criminally responsible.

Concerns abound even though a review conducted by Canadian researchers (see Lymburner & Roesch, 1999) confirmed past findings suggesting that (1) the insanity defence is very rare; (2) it is usually only successful when applied to severely disordered individuals; and (3) people who are found to be insane are still typically detained for long periods of time that may greatly exceed the otherwise appropriate sentence. It is important to note that being found not criminally responsible does not result in an acquittal.

Stone (1975), a professor of law and psychiatry at Harvard University, proposed an intriguing reason for this great interest in finding certain people not guilty by reason of insanity (NGRI or later NCRMD in Canada). Criminal law rests on the assumption that people have free will and that if they do wrong, they have chosen to do so, are blameworthy, and should be punished. Stone suggested that the insanity defence strengthens the concept of free will by pointing to the few people who constitute an exception because they do not have it, namely, those judged to be insane. These individuals are assumed to have less responsibility for their actions because of a mental disorder, an inability to distinguish between right and wrong, or both. They lack the degree of free will that would justify holding them legally accountable for criminal acts. By exclusion, everyone else has free will! "The insanity defence is in every sense the exception that proves the rule. It allows the courts to treat every other defendant as someone who chose 'between good and evil'" (Stone, 1975, p. 222).

LANDMARK CASES IN CANADA In modern Anglo-American criminal law, several court rulings and established principles bear on the problems of legal responsibility and mental illness. Table 18.1 summarizes these rulings and principles.

According to Schneider et al. (2000), Canada's modern history with respect to the legal treatment of mentally disordered people began with the case of Rex v. Hadfield (1800; see Table 18.1). Hadfield fired a shot in the direction of King George III because he believed that the king's death would herald the end of the world and the second advent of Christ (Ogloff & Whittemore, 2001). Hadfield was found not guilty by reason of insanity. This case is noteworthy because the chief justice overseeing the case returned Hadfield to prison but remarked that neither the prison environment nor the community were proper alternatives. This case led the British Parliament to enact the Criminal Lunatics Act (1800), which provided the leeway for people to be sent to a place deemed fit by the court (i.e., a mental institution) rather than be incarcerated or set free. This provision was incorporated into a draft of the British criminal code and the first Criminal Code of Canada in 1892 (see Schneider et al., 2000, for a more complete description).

TABLE 18.1
LANDMARK CASES AND THE DISPOSITION OF THE MENTALLY ILL IN CANADA

CASE	DATE	SIGNIFICANCE
Rex v. Hadfield	1800	Led to changes where mentally ill could be institutionalized rather than returned to prison or community. The accused were held at "His or Her Majesty's Pleasure."
Regina v. M'Naghten	1843	Followed a reference to the House of Lords, setting a standard test for "insanity" that was subsequently adopted, with modifications, by much of the Western world. Is seen to mark the beginning of the modern insanity defence.
Regina v. Chaulk	1990	Specifies that "wrong" means morally wrong as well as legally wrong.
Regina v. Swain	1991	Led to creation of Bill C-30 and establishes the jurisdiction of provincial review boards that can balance the individual's and the community's concerns; changes verdict from "not guilty by reason of insanity" to "not criminally responsible on account of mental disorder."
Regina v. Oommen	1994	The accused must not only be able to know what is wrong but be able to apply that knowledge at the time of the act.
Winko v. British Columbia	1999	If it cannot be determined whether a mentally disordered person is a significant threat to public safety, he or she must be discharged absolutely.

The M'Naghten Rules The well-known criteria, the M'Naghten Rules, were formulated in the aftermath of a murder trial in England in 1843. The accused, Daniel M'Naghten, had set out to kill the British prime minister, Sir Robert Peel, but had mistaken Peel's secretary, Sir Edward Drummond, for Peel. M'Naghten claimed that he had been instructed to kill Lord Peel by the "voice of God." As a result of a post-trial reference to the House of Lords, the M'Naghten Rules were articulated as follows:

> to establish a defence of insanity, it must be clearly proved that, at the time of the committing of the act, the party accused was labouring under such a defect of reason, from disease of the mind, as not to know the nature and quality of the act he was doing; or if he did know it, that he did not know he was doing what was wrong.

The rules are unique in that they were never read as part of a court's ruling at the conclusion of the trial, and they were not part of any legislation. Nevertheless, the M'Naghten Rules have had an unprecedented impact, as they were adopted not only in Britain but throughout all of the Commonwealth and most American jurisdictions as the test to be met in an insanity defence. Prior to the House of Lords' articulation of the law, a defence of insanity could be raised, although different tests were employed in a haphazard, inconsistent manner. A key point to emphasize here is that the M'Naghten Rules apply to insanity at the time of the criminal act or omission.

The issue of being able to tell right from wrong as a component of the insanity defence has been the subject of some debate. According to Ogloff and Whittemore (2001), the Canadian legal system defined "wrong" in terms of legally wrong, but this was expanded by the Supreme Court of Canada in Regina v. Chaulk (1990) to include morally wrong, as well.

The case of Regina v. Swain (1991) led to the proclamation of Bill C-30 on February 4, 1992. Bill C-30 created the mini-code in Part XX.1 within the *Criminal Code of Canada* dealing exclusively with the mentally disordered accused. The case involved a man who had acted in a threatening manner toward members of his family and was subsequently arrested for the crime of assault causing bodily harm. When the police arrived, they discovered that Swain "had swung his children over his head, scored a cross on his wife's chest, spoken about spirits, and fought with the air. At his arrest, he was speaking excitedly in religious themes" (Stuart et al., 2001, p. 528). He later testified that he was trying to save his family from the devil.

Swain recovered after receiving drug treatment and had lived in the community for over a year without incident when the day of his trial finally came. The insanity defence was raised by the Crown over his objections. Swain was found to be NGRI, but according to the Criminal Code provisions, he had to be held in "strict custody," even though he had been out on bail and problem-free at the time of the verdict. The Supreme Court, in reviewing the legislative scheme, found that the failure of the provisions to set a maximum time within which the accused's status must be reviewed constituted a violation of his Charter rights. The court noted that for many other similar situations Parliament had set limits on the amount of time that could pass before an accused's status had to be reviewed. While the case turned on this narrow point, the court expressed "concern" with respect to other features of the legislative scheme. Accordingly, Parliament was given six months to bring the legislation into Charter compliance. This gave birth to Bill C-30.

Bill C-30 included a key change in terminology. The phrase "not guilty by reason of insanity" was altered to "not criminally responsible on account of mental disorder" (NCRMD). Another change concerned the party to be responsible for the individual found NCRMD. Previously, the mentally disordered individual had been kept at the "pleasure" of the lieutenant governor, but now legal authority was allocated to provincial review boards. Ogloff and Whittemore (2001) noted that, prior to changes made to the Criminal Code in 1992, people who were found not guilty by reason of insanity were detained for an indeterminate length of time. However, as a result of Regina v. Swain (1991) and the subsequent proclamation of Bill C-30, review boards now determine the individual's fate within 45 days of the verdict and thereafter not less than annually. Review boards must weigh many factors, including the individual's current mental status and the risk to society posed by the individual. They can discharge the individual with or without conditions, or alternatively, they can order detention in a hospital setting.

Included in Bill C-30 is a list of issues for which assessments may be ordered. The issues include fitness to stand trial, criminal responsibility, infanticide, and, the least onerous, disposition. Specific time limits are set for the assessment of the various issues. It is presumed, for example, that a fitness assessment will be completed within five days, but the maximum period of assessment is set at 60 days for compelling situations. It is also presumed that all assessments will take place out of custody unless the Crown shows why this should not occur. Notwithstanding this presumption, most assessments take place on an in-patient basis because the subject of the assessment is often too unwell to be released into the community. While being assessed, an accused is not to be treated against his or her will. However, if the accused is found to be unfit to stand trial, the Crown may bring an application for the court to order that the accused be treated for up to 60 days in order to render him or her fit. This order, if the evidentiary hurdles are met, will be effected with or without the accused's consent.

Initial research on the impact of Bill C-30 was conducted in British Columbia. A comparison of a cohort of people found NGRI vs. a newer cohort of those found NCRMD uncovered a substantial increase in the number of cases following the enactment of Bill C-30, including a shift toward an increased number of cases involving people charged with less serious offences (Livingston, Wilson, Tien, & Bond, 2003). The average length of hospitalization for the NCRMD cohort (9.8 months) was much lower than for the NGRI cohort (47.7 months). Livingston et al. (2003) concluded, "The Bill C-30 provisions have made the NCRMD defence an attractive option for defendants and legal counsel" (p. 408).

INSANITY AND MENTAL ILLNESS In general, the insanity defence requires applying an abstract principle to specific life situations. As in all aspects of the law, terms can be interpreted in a number of ways—by defendants, defence lawyers, prosecutors, judges, and jurors—and testimony can be presented in a diverse fashion, depending on the skill of the interrogators and the intelligence of the witnesses. Furthermore, because the defendant's mental condition only at the time the crime was committed is in question, retrospective, often speculative, judgement on the part of attorneys, judges, jurors, and psychiatrists is required. And disagreement between defence and prosecution psychiatrists and psychologists is the rule.

A final point should be emphasized. There is an important difference between insanity and mental illness or defect. A person can be diagnosed as mentally ill and yet be held responsible for a crime. Insanity is a legal concept, not a psychiatric or psychological one. And, while the *Criminal Code of Canada* defines "mental disorder"—the legal term—to mean "disease of the mind," the presence of mental disorder is a necessary but not a sufficient condition to make the defence of insanity. This distinction, also a key concept in the U.S. legal system, was made vivid by the 1992 conviction of Jeffrey Dahmer in Wisconsin. He admitted to butchering, cannibalizing, and having sex with the corpses of 15 boys and young men. Dahmer plead guilty but

Insanity is a legal concept and differs from the psychological concept of mental illness. Jeffrey Dahmer, a serial killer and paraphiliac, seemed clearly psychopathological but was not judged insane because he was regarded as knowing right from wrong and as able to control his behaviour.

FITNESS TO STAND TRIAL

The insanity defence concerns the accused person's mental state at the time of the crime. A question that first arises is whether the person is competent or fit to stand trial at all. The mental fitness of individuals to stand trial must be decided before it can be determined whether they are responsible for the crime of which they are accused. The requirement that an accused be fit to stand trial was a refinement of the older principle that an accused had to be present before the state could proceed with its prosecution. The requirement of mere physical presence was expanded to require the accused to be "mentally present" as well. It is possible for a person to be judged competent to stand trial yet subsequently be deemed not criminally responsible by reason of mental disorder. In fact, that is the case for all accused raising the NCRMD defence since they must be fit prior to commencing their trial. Fitness has to do with the accused's present condition, not how he or she might have been functioning at the time of the alleged offence.

Decisions may be changed on appeal if the fitness of the defendant is in question and has not been adequately assessed. For instance, Schneider (2001) related a case in which the Ontario Court of Appeal overturned a conviction for attempted murder because of a judge's failure to assess the fitness of the defendant. In this case, although the Crown attorney suggested to the judge that fitness might be an issue, the judge simply asked the accused whether he felt fit to stand trial (Schneider, 2001). Obviously, fitness needs to be established by trained professionals. Canadian Perspectives 18.1 further examines the fitness to stand trial issue (as well as the use of the insanity defence) in the complex case of Louis Riel.

mentally ill, and his sanity was the sole focus of an unusual trial that had jurors listening to conflicting testimony from mental health experts about the defendant's state of mind during the serial killings to which he had confessed. They had to decide whether he had had a mental disease that prevented him from knowing right from wrong or from being able to control his actions. Even though there was no disagreement that he was mentally ill, diagnosable as having some sort of paraphilia, Dahmer was deemed sane and therefore legally responsible. He was sentenced to 15 consecutive life terms.

CANADIAN PERSPECTIVES 18.1
LOUIS RIEL AND THE ISSUE OF FITNESS TO STAND TRIAL

Louis Riel is one of the most controversial figures in the history of Canada. Riel, of French Canadian and Métis background, was executed for his role in the Métis uprising in 1885 known as the North-West Rebellion. This armed rebellion stemmed from political and land disputes in Western Canada between the Métis and the federal government, and involved the deaths of several North-West Mounted Police. Riel was executed for high treason after a jury found him guilty but recommended mercy.

One vexing question that remains to this day was whether Riel should have been deemed not criminally responsible due to mental disorder. An equally important and related issue is whether he was fit to stand trial. Riel had spent time in mental institutions on two separate occasions prior to the uprising. His lawyers based his defence on the insanity plea, after other options failed, despite his vehement protests that he did not support this strategy.

Was Riel insane at the time of the act or, at the very least, unfit to stand trial because of an inability to participate in his own defence? Riel displayed many symptoms of megalomania (see

Perr, 1992). He believed that he had been specially selected by the spirits to bring forth the message of the Métis. Similar tendencies to put aside one's personal identity and take on another identity (referred to as "misidentification of the self") have come to be described as "The Riel Phenomenon" (see Perr & Federoff, 1992).

The actual documents filed on Riel's behalf by his lawyer, François-Xavier Lemieux, and two psychiatrists contain vivid accounts of Riel's apparent deterioration (Regina v. Louis Riel, 1886). Lemieux noted the following in his declaration:

> While he was speaking he suddenly stops showing me his hand. "Do you see, says he, blood flowing in the veins; the telegraph is operating actively, and I feel it, they are talking about me, and questioning authorities, in Ottawa, about me." It is of similar fantastic visions he speaks with me every day. I am convinced that he is not acting a part, he speaks with a conviction and a sincerity which leave no doubt in my mind about the state of his mind, he has retracted his

errors but he believes himself today to be a prophet and invested with a divine mission to reform the world on the day he has spoken to the Court and when I reprove him for his foolish and extravagant ideas, he answers that he submits, but that he cannot stifle the voice that speaks in him and the spirit that commands him to communicate to the world the revelations he receives. One must have the ferocious hatred of a fanatic or the stupidity of an idiot, to say that Riel is not a fool, because he is intelligent in other matters, as if history was not filled with such anomalies, among certain men who, remarkable in certain subjects, have lost the balance which contains intelligence within the limits from which it cannot escape without losing its privilege of guiding us or making us responsible for our own acts.

...The experience I have gained of this man by continual contact with him has only confirmed me more and more in the opinion I had already formed of him, that he is crazy and insane.... I have just been visiting him, and during an hour he spoke of extraordinary revelations made to him by the spirit the previous night, and that he has been ordered to communicate to me and to all the Catholic clergy: "The great cause of sin in the world is the revolt of the body against the spirit, it is because we do not chew our food enough, and by this want of mastication it communicates animal life only to the body while by masticating and chewing it well, it spiritualizes the body." (Regina v. Louis Riel, p. 204)

The opinion offered by Lemieux was echoed by the two psychiatrists who concluded that Riel was insane and unable to discern right from wrong. However, the medical petition failed and Riel was eventually executed.

THINKING CRITICALLY

1. Was Riel not criminally responsible by reason of mental disorder, or was this simply a desperate attempt on the part of his defence team to avoid his execution? On the basis of your understanding of current legislation, do you think the same sentence and result would have been reached today?

2. Was it ethical of Riel's lawyers and psychiatrists to proceed with the insanity defence against their client's wishes? What would you have done? Note that Riel felt that to argue his insanity would, in effect, undermine the cause of his people and the strength of his views.

Rather than relying on subjective clinical judgements to determine an individual's fitness (or lack of fitness) to stand trial, another alternative is to adopt measures to assist with the decision. One measure developed in Canada is the Fitness Interview Test-Revised (FIT-R; Roesch, Zapf, Webster, & Eaves, 1999). The three components of this interview-based measure assess (1) whether the person understands the nature and purpose of the legal proceedings; (2) whether the person understands the possible or likely consequences of the proceedings; and (3) whether the person is capable of communicating with his or her lawyer. The FIT-R appears to have an exceptional level of validity; for example, a study conducted by Zapf and Roesch (1997) found that the measure resulted in no false negative errors (i.e., it did not call someone fit who is really not fit to stand trial). Subsequent research found that defendants with primary psychotic disorders had greater legal impairment than defendants with other psychiatric disorders in terms of their understanding of various aspects of the legal process and their rights (Viljoen, Roesch, & Zapf, 2002). However, impairment was widespread among other groups, as well. For instance, 27% of those with no diagnosed mental disorder were deemed to have impaired understanding. It seems that IQ level is a key factor; those with higher IQs were less likely to have a problem in understanding. The authors cautioned that a case-by-case functional assessment of legal abilities is required, and special efforts are needed to enhance the legal abilities of all suspects.

What role do psychologists play in fitness and criminal responsibility evaluations in Canada? According to Viljoen, Roesch, Ogloff, and Zapf (2003), psychologists are regarded as qualified to provide assessments under the *Youth Criminal Justice Act* and dangerous offender legislation, but only medical practitioners are qualified to provide court-ordered assessments of fitness and criminal responsibility. However, psychologists often assist physicians by conducting psychological evaluations when requested. Viljoen et al. (2003) predicted that, in time, psychologists will play a larger role in fitness and criminality responsibility evaluations.

Judgements about the fitness to stand trial are still exceedingly difficult at times, and the possible influence of a dissociative state is an issue that further complicates the decision-making process. As noted earlier, in the Dorothy Joudrie case, the determination of a dissociative state was key to the court decision that she was not criminally responsible for shooting her husband. Focus on Discovery 18.1 delves into this issue by summarizing the unusual challenge posed by dissociative identity disorder in criminal commitments.

CIVIL COMMITMENT

Historically, governments have had a duty to protect their citizens from harm. We take for granted the right and duty of government to set limits on our freedom for the sake of protecting us. Few drivers, for example, question the legitimacy

FOCUS ON DISCOVERY 18.1

DISSOCIATIVE IDENTITY DISORDER AND THE INSANITY DEFENCE

Imagine that as you are having a cup of coffee, you hear pounding at the front door. You hurry to answer and find two police officers staring grimly at you. One of them asks, "Are you John Smith?" "Yes," you reply. "Well, sir, you are under arrest for theft and for the murder of Jane Doe." The officer then reads you your rights against self-incrimination, handcuffs you, and takes you to the police station, where you are allowed to call your lawyer. This would be a scary situation for anybody. What is particularly frightening and puzzling is that you have absolutely no recollection of having committed the crime that a detective later describes to you. You are aghast that you cannot account for the time period when the murder was committed; in fact, your memory is startlingly blank for that entire time. And, as if this were not bizarre enough, the detective then shows you a videotape in which you are clearly firing a shotgun at a bank teller during a holdup. "Is that you in the videotape?" asks the detective. You confer with your lawyer, saying that it certainly looks like you, including the clothes, but your lawyer advises you not to admit anything one way or the other.

Let's move forward in time now to your trial some months later. Witnesses have come forward and identified you beyond a reasonable doubt. You know of no one who can testify that you were somewhere other than at the bank on the afternoon of the crimes. And it is clear that the jury is going to find you responsible for the crimes. But did you murder the teller in the bank? You are able to assert honestly to yourself and to the jury that you did not. And yet even you have been persuaded that the person in the videotape is you and that that person committed the robbery and the murder.

Because of the strange nature of the case, your lawyer arranged prior to the trial to have you interviewed by a psychiatrist and a clinical psychologist, both of them well-known experts in forensics. Through extensive questioning, they have decided that you have dissociative identity disorder (DID, formerly called multiple personality disorder) and that the crimes were committed not by you, John Smith, but by your rather violent alter, Dick. Indeed, during one interview, Dick emerged and boasted about the crime, even chuckling because you, John, would be imprisoned for it.

This fictional account is not as far-fetched as you might think. Mental health lawyers have for some time been concerned with such scenarios as they have wrestled with various aspects of the insanity defence, and psychologists are searching for research paradigms that can assist in determining the nature (i.e., validity) of amnesia in legal cases involving DID (see Allen & Iacono, 2001). Note that nearly all the people who successfully use an insanity defence are diagnosable as having schizophrenia (or more generally, as psychotic) and that DID is regarded as a dissociative disorder (and used to be classified as one of the neuroses). Can DID be an excusing condition for a criminal act? Should John Smith be held responsible for a crime committed by his alter, Dick? The quandary is clearly evident in the title of an

The film *Primal Fear* with Richard Gere and Edward Norton portrayed an insanity defence in a case of dissociative identity disorder.

article that addresses the DID issue: "Who's on trial?" (Appelbaum & Greer, 1994).

Consider the legal principle that people accused of crimes should be punished only if they are blameworthy. In reviews of the DID literature and forensic implications, Saks (1997) argues that DID should be regarded as a special case in mental health law, that a new legal principle should be established, "irresponsibility by virtue of multiple personality disorder." Her argument takes issue with legal practice that would hold a person with DID responsible for a crime as long as the personality acting at the time of the crime intended to commit it.

What is intriguing about Saks's argument is that she devotes a major portion of it to defining personhood. What is a person? Is a person the body we inhabit? Well, usually our sense of who we are as persons does not conflict with the bodies we have come to know as our own or, rather, as us. But in DID, there is a discrepancy. The body that committed the crimes at the bank was John Smith. But it was his alter, Dick, who committed the crimes. Saks argues that, peculiar as it may sound, the law should be interested in the body only as a container for the person. It is the person who may or may not be blameworthy, not the body. They are usually one and the same, but in the case of DID, they are not. In a sense, Dick committed the murder by using John's body.

Then is John blameworthy? The person John did not commit the crime; he did not even know about it. Saks argues that it would be unjust for the judge to sentence John, or more specifically, the body in the courtroom who usually goes by that name, because John is descriptively innocent. To be sure, sending John to prison would punish Dick, for whenever he would emerge, he would find himself imprisoned. But what of John? Saks concludes that we cannot imprison John because he is not blameworthy. Rather, we must find him not guilty by reason of DID and remand him for treatment of the disorder.

DID would not, however, be a justification for a verdict of not criminally responsible if the alter that did not commit the crime was aware of the other alter's criminal intent and did not do anything to prevent the criminal act. Under these circumstances, argues Saks, the first alter would be complicit in the crime and blameworthy. Saks draws a comparison to Robert Louis Stevenson's fictional characters of Dr. Jekyll and Mr. Hyde. Jekyll made the potion that caused the emergence of Hyde, his alter, with the foreknowledge that Hyde would do evil. So even though Jekyll was not present when Hyde was in charge, he would nonetheless be blameworthy because of his prior knowledge of what Hyde would do—not to mention that he, Jekyll, had concocted the potion that created his alter, Hyde.

Saks is optimistic about the effectiveness of therapy for DID and believes that people like John/Dick can be integrated into one personality and then released to rejoin society. Saks goes so far as to argue that people with DID who are judged dangerous but who have not committed a crime should be subject to civil commitment, even though this would be tantamount to preventive detention. In this way, she suggests, future crimes might be avoided.[1]

[1] It should be recalled that a substantial number of mental health professionals dispute the existence of DID. For them, Saks's arguments would not be persuasive.

of imposing limits on them by providing traffic signals that often make them stop when they would rather go. Government has a long-established right as well as an obligation to protect us both from ourselves—the *parens patriae*, "power of the state"—and from others—the police power of the state. Civil commitment is one further exercise of these powers.

In virtually all jurisdictions, a person can be committed to a psychiatric hospital against his or her will if a judgement is made that he or she is (1) mentally ill and (2) a danger to self (i.e., unable to provide for the basic physical needs of food, clothing, and shelter) or a danger to others (Perlin, 1994). (There is also a form of outpatient commitment, which we describe later.)

Specific commitment procedures generally fit into one of two categories: formal or informal. Formal or judicial commitment is by order of a court. It can be requested by any responsible citizen; usually the police, a relative, or a friend seeks the commitment. If the judge believes that there is a good reason to pursue the matter, he or she will order a mental health examination. The person has the right to object to these attempts to "certify" him or her, and a court hearing can be scheduled to allow the person to present evidence against commitment. In Canada, this procedure is covered by provincial legislation that permits an *ex parte* hearing before a justice of the peace. Generally, this legislation permits a justice of the peace to have an individual held against his or her will a period of time (e.g. up to 72 hours in Ontario) for the purposes of assessment only. If, after that period of assessment, the individual meets the certification criteria, she or he may be held for longer periods, and most provinces have a process for subsequent involuntary treatment. Alternatively, where the prospective patient is compliant, a person may be brought to a physician who may, where the individual is seen as a danger to him/herself or to others, issue the same process. For example, in Ontario the form signed by the physician (Form 1) is in effect for seven days and is authority for a peace officer to take the individual to a psychiatric facility for assessment for up to 72 hours. If seven days elapse, and an order of a physician or justice of the peace has not been effected, it is no longer valid.

Informal, emergency commitment of mentally ill persons can be accomplished without initially involving the courts. For example, if a hospital administrative board believes that a voluntary patient requesting discharge is too disturbed and

dangerous to be released, it can detain the patient with a temporary, informal commitment order.

Civil commitment affects far more people than criminal commitment. It is beyond the scope of this book to examine the intricacies of civil commitment laws. Our aim is to present an overview that will provide a basic understanding of the issues and current directions of change.

Table 18.2 provides an overview of the current Canadian criteria for involuntary admission for the provinces and territories (see Gray & O'Reilly, 2001). Inspection of this table reveals considerable differences among the provinces in the criteria used. One overarching difference is that some jurisdictions use a broad definition of mental disorder, while others use a specific definition. Douglas and Koch (2001) noted that provinces with a specific definition actually use a functional definition of mental illness that is quite detailed. The definition of mental disorder in Saskatchewan, for example, is "a disorder of thought, perceptions, feelings or behaviour that seriously impairs a person's judgment, capacity to recognize reality, ability to associate with others or ability to meet the ordinary demands of life, in which respect treatment is available" (Douglas & Koch, 2001, p. 355). In contrast, Ontario, Quebec, Nova Scotia, and Newfoundland and Labrador do not use such precise and detailed definitions of the impact of mental illness. In Ontario, mental disorder is defined simply as "a disease or disability of the mind" (see Douglas & Koch, 2001, p. 355).

The provinces and territories also differ in how they define harm to self or others. Ontario, Alberta, and the Northwest Territories and Nunavut focus on a definition that emphasizes the possibility of physical harm. Douglas and Koch (2001) state that Alberta is particularly stringent in its conceptualization of dangerousness. Other jurisdictions have an expanded definition of harm that includes the possibility of a wider range of harmful acts that may or may not involve direct physical damage involving the self or others. Gray and O'Reilly (2001) note that four provinces include the additional criterion that the person is deemed likely to suffer further deterioration, either mental or physical.

The column on the far right of Table 18.2 shows that, at present, Saskatchewan is distinct in that even if other criteria are satisfied, individuals are not committed in this province if they are capable of making a treatment decision. Gray and O'Reilly

TABLE 18.2

CANADIAN CRITERIA FOR INVOLUNTARY ADMISSION BY JURISDICTION

JURISDICTION	DEFINITION OF MENTAL DISORDER	HARM CRITERION	DETERIORATION AS ALTERNATIVE TO HARM	NEED FOR TREATMENT	NOT CAPABLE OF TREATMENT DECISION
British Columbia	Specific	Broad	Yes	Yes	No
Alberta	Specific	Physical	No	No	No
Saskatchewan	Specific	Broad	Yes	Yes	Yes
Manitoba	Specific	Broad	Yes	Yes	No
Ontario	Broad	Physical ?	Yes	Yes & No[†]	No
Quebec	Broad	?	No	No	No
New Brunswick	Specific	Broad	No	Implied	No
Nova Scotia	Broad	?	No	Implied	No
Prince Edward Island	Specific	Broad	No	Implied	No
Newfoundland and Labrador	Broad	Broad	No	Implied	No
Yukon	Specific	Broad	No	No	No
Northwest Territories & Nunavut	Specific	Physical	No	No	No

? Not clear from the legislation or court cases how to classify.
[†] "Yes" for deterioration and "no" for bodily harm.
Adapted with permission from Gray & O'Reilly (2001)

(2001) indicated that this caveat exists to rule out situations in which a person is committed but then refuses the treatment needed in order to recover and eventually be discharged.

Who experiences civil commitment in Canada? Crisanti and Love (2001) examined admissions at the Department of Psychiatry at Calgary General Hospital for the years 1987 to 1995. Involuntary commitment was more likely to apply to males (54%); those who were committed involuntarily had substantially longer hospital stays than voluntary people; and involuntarily committed people were also more likely to be diagnosed with schizophrenia and be known to the justice system.

COMMUNITY COMMITMENT: COMMUNITY TREATMENT ORDERS

> "I have patients who, if they weren't on CTOs, they would tell me 'I don't want to see you Doc.' They wouldn't turn up for their appointments. They wouldn't take their medications and there'd be nothing I could do about it."
> —from Foot, 2007, May 26

One controversial issue that has arisen in Canada involves the concepts of involuntary community commitment and community treatment orders (CTOs). The latter, introduced in Chapter 1, can be characterized as a form of community commitment designed to ensure treatment compliance. In July 1995, Saskatchewan was the first province to implement CTOs (see Goering et al., 2000; O'Reilly, Keegan, & Elias, 2000), followed by Ontario in 2000. Legislation for CTOs was passed in Nova Scotia in 2005 to be enacted in July of 2007. CTOs are also under consideration in Alberta and Newfoundland and Labrador. CTOs stipulate that the individual will be released back into the community only if he or she adheres to

recommended treatments. It is a controversial topic because this condition of release essentially forces people to be treated, regardless of their wishes. Foot (2007) outlines the story of Glen Race, a 26-year-old from Nova Scotia who was wanted for the murders of two men in Halifax and a third in New York state. His family, who stated that he has struggled with paranoid schizophrenia for six years, indicated that they tried everything to get additional treatment for him, but they were unsuccessful. They issued a statement in May 2007 that his alleged killing spree could have been prevented if Nova Scotia had CTOs. Race was captured in Texas earlier in May 2007.

In Saskatchewan, several criteria must be met in order for a CTO to be invoked (see O'Reilly et al., 2000):

Glen Douglas Race from Nova Scotia apparently suffers from paranoid schizophrenia. His parents claimed that he wouldn't have killed three men in 2007 if Nova Scotia's CTO legislation had been in effect. In a public letter they stated that, "we, too, have lost a loved one."

1. The person must have a mental disorder that requires treatment and the treatment can be provided in the community.
2. The person has received in-patient involuntary treatment for 60 cumulative days or more, has been in an in-patient facility on three or more occasions in the last two years, or has previously been the subject of a CTO.
3. The person may harm themselves or others or suffer from physical deterioration without care or supervision.
4. Services must exist in the community and must be available.
5. The person is unable to understand or is incapable of making an informed decision about the need for care and treatment as a result of his or her mental disorder.
6. The person is capable of complying with the requirements of a CTO.

According to the Centre for Addiction and Mental Health (CAMH), 63 CTOs were given in Saskatchewan over a three-year period (from a population of 6,000 people with serious mental illness) and 95% of people in Saskatchewan with a CTO had a diagnosis of schizophrenia (CAMH Best Advice Paper, 2000). A survey of Saskatchewan psychiatrists found that 62% were satisfied or extremely satisfied with the effects of CTOs on their patients, while only 10% were dissatisfied or extremely dissatisfied. However, CTOs are issued for only three months in Saskatchewan (as opposed to six months in Ontario), and survey respondents felt that the three-month period was too short (see O'Reilly et al., 2000).

The law establishing CTOs in Ontario came into effect on December 1, 2000. It is named "Brian's Law" in memory of a popular Ottawa sportscaster who was killed by a man with paranoid schizophrenia who did not adhere to his prescribed treatment. Critics called it the "leash law" and some claimed that the police would soon drag the mentally ill away in handcuffs if they refused medication. The CTO criteria in Ontario differ slightly from those in Saskatchewan. A CTO may be issued if the person has two admissions or 30 cumulative days as an in-patient over a three-year period (see Gray & O'Reilly, 2001). Thus, the provinces differ in the specific CTO details. Although concerns have been raised about the coercive aspects of CTOs, it is interesting that the Province of Ontario, in describing the legislation, still maintains that all protections involving the issue of informed consent still exist. Also, according to this legislation (see Brian's Law [Mental Health Legislative Reform], 2000), individuals subjected to a CTO retain a number of rights, including

1. a right of review by the Consent and Capacity Board with appeal to the courts each time a CTO is issued or reviewed;
2. a mandatory review by the Consent and Capacity Board every second time a CTO is reviewed;
3. a right to request a re-examination by the issuing physician to determine if the CTO is still needed in order for the person to live in the community; and

4. a right of review of finding of incapacity to consent to treatment.

In Ontario, the procedure should really be referred to as a "community treatment agreement" because the patient is free to withdraw his or her consent at any time. When that is done, the "order" comes to an end.

Richard O'Reilly (2004) from the University of Western Ontario concluded that few issues have so polarized the stakeholders in the mental health system as CTOs. Table 18.3 summarizes his analysis of the major arguments for and against CTOs.

It should be noted that in Canadian jurisdictions, in contrast to many other countries, a requirement for previous hospitalization for compulsory community treatment precludes

---

TABLE 18.3

ARGUMENTS SUPPORTING AND AGAINST CTOs

SUPPORTING CTOs

1. CTOs are a predictable and acceptable consequence of deinstitutionalization.
2. Society has a *parens patriae* obligation to care for citizens who cannot care for themselves.
3. Lack of awareness of mental illness is a persistent symptom for many patients.
4. Offering services is often not enough when patients lack insight.
5. The assumption that physicians can safely manage patients by committing them just at the point they become dangerous is mistaken.
6. CTOs are less restrictive than involuntary hospitalization.
7. Research confirms the effectiveness of CTOs.
8. No evidence indicates negative effects of CTOs.

AGAINST CTOs

1. Society should never coerce individuals to take treatment.
2. CTOs extend coercion into the community.
3. It is more difficult to protect patients' rights in the community.
4. If we had sufficient services we would not need CTOs.
5. Coercion will be used as an alternative to providing adequate service.
6. People should not be coerced to accept services when there are others willing to accept, but who cannot access, them.
7. People often refuse medications because of side effects or other bona fide reasons.
8. Research on CTOs is inconclusive.
9. CTOs will be used to sweep undesirable individuals off the streets.
10. Hospitals will fill up with non-adherent patients.
11. Coercion drives people away from the mental health system.

Adapted from O'Reilly (2004, p. 580). Reprinted with permission from the Canadian Psychiatric Association.

the use of CTOs with first episode patients (see Gray & O'Reilly, 2005). Some other jurisdictions (e.g., New Zealand) require that compulsory psychiatric treatment be delivered in the least restrictive setting—the community—and hospitalization can be ordered only if community treatment is inappropriate.

Conditional leave from hospital is another form of a compulsory community treatment provision in Canadian mental health acts (see Gray & O'Reilly, 2005, for a review). It is a mechanism that allows a patient who continues to meet committal criteria to live in the community if he or she adheres to specified conditions. Seven of the 12 Canadian mental health acts (British Columbia, Alberta, Manitoba, New Brunswick, Yukon, Prince Edward Island, and Ontario) have conditional leave provisions that differ somewhat in pre-conditions, renewal, and consent (see Gray & O'Reilly, 2005, for a full discussion). For example, Manitoba, Prince Edward Island, and the Yukon require consent, whereas in the other jurisdictions the leave is authorized by the hospital. By definition, a conditional leave has to involve at least one hospital admission, which could be the first one. Manitoba requires multiple hospitalizations (identical to Saskatchewan for CTOs). In Quebec a judge can authorize treatment that can extend into the community after discharge.

What are the consequences of a patient's non-adherence to the conditions of a community treatment provision? As noted by Gray and O'Reilly (2005), either the person can be apprehended and examined involuntarily to determine if involuntary admission is warranted (e.g., Ontario) or returned directly to hospital without a re-examination of admissibility (e.g., British Columbia).

The issue of whether a CTO is issued and how it is implemented depends greatly on the clinician's determination of whether it is warranted. Dawson (2006) observed that mental health legislation provides only a legal framework and that jurisdictions differ greatly in how often CTOs are used. He noted that CTOs are quite common in Australia and New Zealand and in the District of Columbia in the U.S., but that they are used relatively little in Canada.

There is a relative lack of research on the impact of CTOs in Canada, but extensive research has been conducted in those American states that have implemented CTOs. By and large, these investigations point to the benefits of CTOs. For example, an investigation in North Carolina by Swanson et al. (2001) found that patients who received long-term outpatient commitment had lower probabilities of being arrested than a comparison group, and the key factor accounting for this outcome was a reduced risk of violent behaviour. A study conducted over a three-year period at the Royal Ottawa Hospital yielded very favourable findings (see O'Brien & Farrell, 2005). CTOs were associated with significant reductions in the number and length of hospital admissions and contributed to greater use of community supports, including available housing. The lack of CTOs in Nova Scotia is why a team of researchers interested in the

consequences and benefits of CTOs compared CTO cases from Western Australia with cases from Nova Scotia (see Kisely, Smith, Preston, & Xiao, 2005). Comparisons of matched cases showed that compulsory community treatment did not reduce the risk of hospital readmission, and, in fact, CTO cases actually had a greater readmission rate. However, the authors noted that this could have been due to the fact that CTO cases actually had greater scrutiny and constant evaluation, as well as the general fact that readmission rates are lower in Nova Scotia than in Australia.

O'Reilly et al. (2006) conducted a qualitative study of 26 CTO cases from Regina and Saskatoon. The most predominant diagnoses were schizophrenia and schizoaffective disorder. This study involved interviews of patients, clinicians, family members, and community members. Patients were generally favourable but somewhat ambivalent; they resented the coercion but this wore off over time in most instances, and many patients recognized the need for structure and support that came as a result of the CTO. Still, a small subset of patients remained resentful of the coercion. Family members and clinicians were much less ambivalent; family members were very positive about the CTO and most clinicians saw the CTOs as helpful for most patients. However, they suggested that the three-month duration is too short and should be extended to at least six months. This suggestion fits with the results of an earlier American study that found that CTO treatment was more effective if treatment was maintained for at least 180 days with seven or more sessions per month (see Swartz et al., 2001).

Churchill and Owen (2007) reviewed 72 empirical studies from six countries, including Canada, and concluded that it could not be determined one way or the other whether CTOs benefit or harm patients. Many questions remain unanswered in the CTO debate. As noted by Chaimowitz (2004), "the data, helpful as they may be, can be used selectively by both sides of the CTO debate" (p. 578). Less forceful alternatives, such as assertive community treatment teams, do exist. It will be important to demonstrate that CTOs are more effective than alternatives if their continued use is to be justified. In Ontario numerous new community resources were made available when the government imposed Brian's Law (Foot, 2007). Thus, community-based resource staff can ensure that patients take their medication, help them find housing and jobs, or enroll them in community services. Perhaps the advent of CTOs will facilitate the development of comprehensive therapeutic community mental health systems that are well funded and resourced.

Clearly, simply issuing a CTO or conditional leave is not a solution. It must be followed through with the provision of high-quality care. This was illustrated in another recent tragic example. Seung Hui Cho killed 32 students and faculty members, and then himself, at Virginia Technical University on April 16, 2007. Further examination revealed that a CTO was issued for Cho in 2005 after he stalked and harassed two students and it was determined that he had suicidal and violent thoughts. Cho was ordered into outpatient community treatment after a judge deemed that he was an imminent danger to himself. However, Cho never received treatment because he was never contacted by community services. Accordingly, the gaps in psychiatric care are now being reviewed in hearings conducted by the Virginia House of Delegates (Craig & Jenkins, 2007).

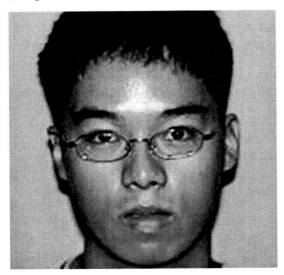

Seung Hui Cho killed 32 students and faculty at Virginia Tech in 2007. Despite the fact a CTO had been issued, he never received treatment.

PREVENTIVE DETENTION AND PROBLEMS IN RISK ASSESSMENT

The perception is widespread that mentally ill people account for a significant proportion of the violence that besets contemporary society, but this is not the case (e.g., Bonta, Law, & Hanson, 1998; Monahan, 1992). Although the issue is complex, and the two constructs are positively related, "the relative contribution of mental illness to the overall rate of violence in society is quite small" (Norko & Baranoski, 2005, p. 21). Only about 3% of the violence in the United States is linked clearly to mental illness (Swanson, Holzer, Ganju, & Jono, 1990). Moreover, about 90% of people diagnosed as psychotic (primarily schizophrenic) are not violent (Swanson et al., 1990). Mentally ill persons—even allowing for their relatively small numbers—do not account for a large proportion of violent offenders, especially when compared with substance abusers and people who are in their teens and twenties, male, and poor (Mulvey, 1994). Large community-based studies indicate that mental disorders do increase violence risk when they co-occur with substance abuse (Monahan et al., 2001; Swanson et al., 1990). However, one study suggests that former mental health patients who are not substance abusers are no more likely to engage in violence than are non-mentally ill individuals who are not substance abusers. Thus, if substance abuse is not involved, mentally ill people are no more prone to violence than the average person. Also, when former patients do act aggressively, it is usually against family

members or friends and the incidents tend to occur at home (Steadman et al., 1998). By and large, then, the general public is seldom affected by violence from former mental health patients. Thus, certain case studies outlined in this chapter are atypical in the sense that they involve violent and aggressive acts committed by people with mental disorders.

Nevertheless, there is a strong connection in the public mind between violence and mental illness, and this belief is central to society's justification of civil commitment (e.g., Steadman et al., 1998), as well as to the stigma attached to having been a patient in a psychiatric institution (e.g., Steadman et al., 1998). In fact, there is some evidence that mental disorder may sometimes contribute to violence, enough to justify preventive detention. In the Steadman et al. (1998) study, for example, substance abuse increased the chances of violent behaviour more among discharged mental health patients than among non-patient controls. There is also accumulating evidence that the effect of psychosis on risk of violence is much greater for women than for men. For example, Dean et al. (2006) reported that the two-year prevalence of physical assault in a community-dwelling sample of British women with chronic psychosis was 17%. Assaultive behaviour in these women was associated with previous violence, non-violent convictions, victimization, African-Caribbean ethnicity, cluster B personality disorder, and high levels of unmet need. Skeem et al. (2006) conducted an intensive study of psychiatric emergency room patients at high risk for community violence based on an actuarial prediction model. Patients with a diagnosis of schizophrenia or current report of delusions were excluded. The authors evaluated prospectively the temporal relation between symptoms and violence and reported that a high-risk patient with increased anger in one week is more likely to be involved in serious violence the following week. Violence was not related to anxiety, depression, or delusional beliefs. We now examine the issues and the evidence in greater detail.

THE PREDICTION OF DANGEROUSNESS The likelihood of committing an act that is dangerous to the self or others is central to civil commitment. Historically, the focus of assessment has been on the prediction of dangerousness, but more contemporary approaches focus on the assessment of risk rather than the prediction of dangerousness (see Lyon, Hart, & Webster, 2001). Lyon et al. (2001) attribute the shift in emphasis to several factors, including results indicating that professionals tended to overestimate the incidence of violence when the institutionalized were released. Moreover, a focus on the dangerousness inherent in the individual promotes a tendency to attribute outcomes entirely to the dispositional traits of the individual and fails to take into account circumstantial and situational factors.

Regardless of which term is used, is dangerousness easily predicted or is risk easily assessed? Early studies examining the accuracy of predictions that a person would commit a dangerous act found that mental health professionals were poor at making this judgement (e.g., Kozol, Boucher, &

Garofalo, 1972). Collectively, there is extensive literature on the limited validity of clinical judgements, including several studies conducted in Canada (e.g., Menzies & Webster, 1995). A meta-analytic, quantitative review by Hanson and Bussière (1998) found that the ability of clinicians to predict recidivism among sex offenders is only slightly better than chance. The low validity of these judgements is a serious problem because of the weight given to such information. In fact, a Canadian study found that the senior clinician's testimony was the strongest predictor of the decision reached by tribunals in deciding whether to continue to detain forensic patients in maximum security (Hilton & Simmons, 2001).

One alternative is to make decisions on the basis of actuarial prediction. Actuarial prediction involves the use of statistical formulae composed of factors that are significant predictors of dangerousness. The factors are weighted statistically by their importance, based on the outcomes of previous studies. Several actuarial measures have been developed in Canada to assist decision-makers. The PCL-R (Hare, 1991), discussed in Chapter 13, is a consistent predictor of criminal recidivism (see Heilbrun, Ogloff, & Picarrello, 1999) and is often included in risk assessment batteries, either as a stand-alone measure or as part of a broader assessment battery.

Lyon et al. (2001) summarized the strengths and criticisms of the actuarial approach. First, actuarial assessments are more likely than clinical ratings to use quantitative ratings and less likely to be influenced by subjective biases. Second, actuarial measures involve greater consistency because the creators of the measures have already specified with precision the information involved, the strategies for data coding, and required analyses. Also, according to Lyon et al., actuarial decisions are easy for others to review. However, these same authors note that actuarial approaches may be too rigid and cannot be altered to take into account individual factors of potential importance. In addition, actuarial measures are derived from specific populations, so the generalizability of statistical formulae to other populations is always an issue.

Lyon et al. (2001) noted that another alternative that is growing in popularity is to rely on more structured forms of clinical judgements instead of unstructured clinical judgements or actuarial approaches. The HCR-20 is a more structured assessment device developed in Canada (see Webster, Douglas, Eaves, & Hart, 1997). "HCR" refers to historical variables, clinical variables, and risk variables. Historical variables include such factors as previous violence, early maladjustment at home or at school, history of serious mental disorder, and other personality disorders. Current clinical variables include such indicators as being unresponsive to treatment, a lack of insight, and acting in an impulsive manner. Finally, additional risk variables include consideration of such factors as lack of social support and experience of stressful events.

Quinsey, Harris, Rice, and Cormier (1998) criticized the HCR-20 on the grounds that it includes certain factors (e.g., a history of serious mental disorder) that have not been robust predictors of risk in previous studies. Moreover, they observed that the HCR-20 is not an actuarial measure in the truest

sense because the checklist items were not selected on the basis of empirical links with outcomes. The assessment package they advocate using is described in Canadian Contributions 18.1, which examines the contributions of Marnie Rice.

Regardless of the criticism, a growing number of studies attest to the predictive usefulness of the HCR-20. For instance, the HCR-20 is better than the PCL-R at postdicting previous acts of violence and antisocial behaviour in incarcerated offenders (Douglas & Webster, 1999). Note that postdiction involves the identification of variables that are found, after the fact, to distinguish violent tendencies. Another study by Douglas, Ogloff, Nicholls, and Grant (1999) demonstrated that the HCR-20 had predictive validity in terms of predicting subsequent acts of violence in civilly committed patients, and once again, the HCR-20 outperformed the PCL-R screening version.

An investigation conducted in the United Kingdom showed that even though the PCL-R had moderate predictive ability, the HCR-20 outperformed it in terms of subsequent acts of verbal aggression, physical aggression, and violence to property (Gray et al., 2003). However, Gray et al. (2003) also noted that studies with the HCR-20 have been conducted with psychiatric patients and, thus far, no study has been conducted with non-mentally disordered prisoners. In another British study, Doyle and Dolan (2006) assessed patients discharged from both forensic and non-forensic psychiatric services and followed up at 24 weeks post discharge. They reported that historical measures of risk and measures of psychopathy, impulsiveness, and anger were highly predictive of community violence. Doyle and Dolan (2006) concluded that the HCR-20 was the most robust predictor of violence. Further, the clinical and risk management items (which are more dynamic or changeable) added incremental validity to the risk assessment over and above the static historical factors. Of course, as noted by Wynn (2006), even validated instruments such as the HCR-20 may not be helpful in predicting first episodes of violence because, to a large extent, they draw on the history of violence. Elbogen et al. (2006) also assessed malleable, dynamic factors in addition to static factors in outpatients with mental disorders from five sites in the United States. Community violence was inversely related to treatment adherence, perceived treatment need, and perceived treatment effectiveness.

A court decision in the case of Winko v. British Columbia (see Table 18.1) further increases the importance of making accurate risk assessments. This case established that where there is uncertainty about whether an offender poses a risk, the onus is on the province in question to resolve this uncertainty, and if it cannot be resolved, the former offender must be released (see Schneider et al., 2000). In other words, unless the provincial review board can find affirmatively that the accused poses a significant threat to the safety of the public, he or she must be discharged absolutely. Previously, the interpretation of the law was that if there was uncertainty about risk, then the person in question would remain subject to the jurisdiction of the provincial review board.

Parenthetically, another aspect of this case involved the issue of "capping provisions" and setting a standard for the maximum amount of time that a person could be detained. The issue was whether Winko and three other offenders with similar appeals could be detained, perhaps indefinitely, if risk of dangerousness was still evident (see Schneider et al., 2000). The court ruled that these individuals could indeed still be held if there was a risk of dangerousness, with the caveat mentioned above that the risk of dangerousness had to be demonstrated.

CANADIAN CONTRIBUTIONS 18.1
MARNIE RICE AND ACTUARIAL RISK ASSESSMENT

Marnie Rice was made a fellow of the Royal Society of Canada in 2003. She has been a vital member of an effective research team based at the Oak Ridge Mental Health Centre in Penetanguishene, Ontario. Other team members include Grant Harris, Vernon Quinsey, and Catherine Cormier. Rice is the former Director of Research at the centre and, upon her retirement, now holds the title of Director of Research Emerita. Her collaborative work has contributed greatly to our understanding of forensic patients and risk assessment, and in recognition of this, she was the 1995 recipient of the American Psychological Association Award for Contribution to Research in Public Policy. She was given the award for "pioneering the rigorous empirical evaluation of risk assessment and risk reduction in difficult forensic populations. . . . With her colleagues Grant Harris and Vernon Quinsey, she has established a remarkable program of cutting-edge research on the actuarial assessment of violence risk" (American Psychological Association, 1996, p. 342). She has also studied social skills deficits and clinical treatment, and she developed a program for preventing institutional violence.

Marnie Rice has furthered the actuarial approach to risk assessment.

Rice and her colleagues developed the Violence Risk Appraisal Guide (VRAG; Rice & Harris, 1995) for the purposes of actuarial assessments of risk, that is, using statistical models to predict the likelihood of violence. The construction and development of the VRAG is described at length in Quinsey et al. (1998). Rice and her associates hoped to create an assessment tool that could predict over time which institutionalized offenders would incur another criminal charge from a violent act after being released. The 12 variables that compose the VRAG are displayed in Table 18.4. This table indicates that the two best predictors within the VRAG are scores on the PCL-R (Hare, 1991) and a variable of elementary school maladjustment. The negative correlation between violent recidivism and age at the time of the index offence indicates that risk is higher to the extent that the offender was relatively young. Similarly, the negative correlation with schizophrenia indicates that it is associated with less risk (also see Rice & Harris, 1995) and underscores one of the main findings emerging from the work of Rice and her associates, namely, that mental disorder per se is not a risk factor. In fact, Rice (1997) concluded that "violent recidivism among mentally disordered individuals is related to the same variables as among non-mentally disordered individuals" (p. 420), so there is no basis for public perceptions that link mental disorder with the possibility of violence.

A comparative study found that the VRAG predicted general recidivism, as well as sexual and violent recidivism, thus supporting the actuarial approach (Barbaree, Seto, Langston, & Peacock, 2001). Prospective research involving a five-year follow-up of the original cohort of forensic patients found that the VRAG was a strong predictor of violent recidivism and a robust predictor of extreme violence (Harris, Rice, & Cormier, 2002). Comparative research of four actuarial measures found that the VRAG was comparable or superior to these measures in predicting violent recidivism and sexually motivated recidivism (Harris et al., 2003). Finally, in a very specific context, Rice and Harris (2003) found that the VRAG was a good predictor of violent and sexual recidivism by father-daughter child molesters, even though it was the case that these child molesters had lower scores on the VRAG and lower rates of recidivism than non-familial child molesters.

A general finding that has emerged from research conducted in Canada is that it is the psychopaths among us who are especially likely to reoffend in a violent manner (see Rice & Harris, 1995; Serin & Amos, 1995). Rice (1997) is quite pessimistic about the chances of treating and rehabilitating the psychopaths who have participated in her research investigations, in part because some findings indicate that treatment actually yields worse outcomes. For these people, treatment is a chance to improve their social skills and increase their charm in order to further mislead unsuspecting victims. As a result, Rice decided to concentrate her efforts on developing measures such as the VRAG that may be used to identify these people, so members of the court and review boards will be aware of whom they are evaluating. Evidence continues to attest to the validity of the measure. For instance, Rice and Harris (1997) showed that the VRAG predicted violent recidivism among sex offenders. One extension of work in this area is a version of the VRAG designed specifically for sex offenders, the Sex Offenders Risk Appraisal Guide (SORAG; see Quinsey et al., 1998).

TABLE 18.4

VIOLENCE RISK APPRAISAL GUIDE (VRAG) VARIABLES AND PEARSON CORRELATIONS WITH VIOLENT RECIDIVISM

Revised Psychopathy Checklist score	.34
Elementary school maladjustment score	31
Meets *DSM-III* criteria for any personality disorder	.26
Age at the time of the index offence	−.26
Separation from either parent (except death) under age 16	.25
Failure on prior conditional release	.24
Non-violent offence history score (using the Cormier-Lang scale)	.20
Never married (or equivalent)	.18
Meets *DSM-III* criteria for schizophrenia	−.17
Most serious victim injury (from the index offence)	−.16
Alcohol abuse score	.13
Female victim in the index offence	−.11

Adapted from Quinsey et al. (1988, p. 147), Exhibit 8.1. Reprinted with permission from the American Psychological Association.

Litwack (2001) concluded that the VRAG is the best actuarial tool for assessing dangerousness to date. Still, significant concerns remain. First, we are still a long way from being able to use actuarial measures to determine levels of dangerousness with absolute certainty. The correlation between the VRAG and the outcome measure of violent recidivism is approximately $r = .44$ (see Rice, 1997), which means that almost four fifths of the variance in this important outcome measure still remains to be predicted. Violence is a product of the individual's personal characteristics (including the consumption of drugs and/or alcohol) and the environment within which he or she is functioning. To make the point, you could take two clinically similar individuals with identical VRAG scores and place them in two very different environments:

one will possibly reoffend, whereas the other possibly will not. Much of the variance in violent recidivism is accounted for by environmental factors that are probably not captured by instruments such as the VRAG. Second, although Litwack (2001) concluded that the VRAG is the best assessment device available, he feels that it must receive more validation in order to be used to make the important decision of whether a person should be detained because of his or her dangerousness. Third, as a general criticism of the actuarial approach, Rogers (2000) noted that current measures are limited by their focus on negative predictors involving risk instead of protective factors that increase an offender's resilience when back in society.

Finally, proponents of the HCR-20 believe that it is more suitable because it includes an assessment of dynamic, changing clinical risk factors. In addition, these researchers emphasize the importance of a multi-faceted approach that incorporates actuarial assessment within a model that also includes structured clinical judgements by trained professionals (Douglas, Ogloff, & Hart, 2003). Rice, Harris, and Quinsey (2002), however, have suggested that while dynamic predictors help predict when an individual is likely to offend or reoffend, they are of limited usefulness in determining who is at greatest risk of offending.

The prediction of dangerousness remains a complicated and very difficult enterprise. Nevertheless, the work and contributions of Marnie Rice and her colleagues has illustrated the potential usefulness of actuarial measures. In an overview of the VRAG research program, Bloom, Webster, Hucker, and De Freitas (2005) listed 10 contemporary risk assessment principles and reiterated the need to adhere to the duty to protect. The fifth principle is especially relevant: actuarial information obtained from records can focus and strengthen risk assessments and additional pertinent information can come to light as the VRAG is being completed. Finally, in a recent paper, Rice and her colleagues (Hilton, Harris, & Rice, 2006) expressed concern about the common failure of clinicians to use the actuarial approach despite evidence of its usefulness and reiterated that it should be used in contexts where it makes sense to do so. They are particularly concerned about new models and approaches that do not make use of actuarial assessments and represent a return to a reliance on clinical judgements. Nonetheless, as noted by Doyle and Dolan (2006), the VRAG is probably a better predictor in populations that have a history of offending behaviour.

Some researchers have gone so far as to argue that civil commitment for the purposes of preventive detention should be abolished. Reconsideration of earlier research suggests that greater accuracy can be achieved in predicting dangerousness in the longer term (e.g., Steadman et al., 1998). Violence prediction becomes more accurate under the following conditions (note the role played by situational factors, sometimes in interaction with personality variables) (e.g., Campbell, Stefan, & Loder, 1994):

- If a person has been repeatedly violent in the recent past, it is reasonable to predict that he or she will be violent in the near future unless there have been major changes in the

person's attitudes or environment. Thus, if a violent person is placed in a restrictive environment, such as a prison or high-security psychiatric hospital facility, he or she may well not be violent, given the markedly changed environment.

- If violence is in the person's distant past and constituted a single but very serious act, and if that person has been incarcerated for a period of time, then violence can be expected on release if there is reason to believe that the person's predetention personality and physical abilities have not changed and the person is going to return to the same environment in which he or she was previously violent.

- Even with no history of violence, violence can be predicted if the person is judged to be on the brink of a violent act, for example, if the person is pointing a loaded gun at an occupied building.

In addition, as stated earlier, the presence of substance abuse significantly raises the rate of violence (Steadman et al., 1998). This finding supports the inclusion of substance abuse among the factors to be considered when attempting to predict violence. (Substance abuse predicts violence also among non-mentally disordered individuals [Gendreau, Little, & Goggin, 1996].) Violence in discharged mental health patients is usually attributable to that small percentage of individuals who do not take their medication or, possibly, who self-medicate (Elbogen et al., 2006; Monahan, 1992). Outpatient commitment is one way to increase medication compliance.

For a detailed discussion of the responsibility of therapists to predict dangerousness, see Focus on Discovery 18.2.

FOCUS ON DISCOVERY 18.2
THE TARASOFF CASE—THE DUTY TO WARN AND TO PROTECT

The client's right to privileged communication—the legal right of a client to require that what goes on in therapy remain confidential—is an important protection, but it is not absolute. Society has long stipulated certain conditions in which confidentiality in a relationship should not be maintained because of harm that can befall others. A famous California court ruling in 1974[2] described circumstances in which a therapist not only may but must breach the sanctity of a client's communication. The facts in this case are outlined below:

IN 1968, Prosenjit Poddar, a graduate student from India studying at the University of California at Berkeley, met Tatiana (Tanya) Tarasoff at a folk dancing class. They saw each other weekly during the fall, and she kissed him on New Year's Eve. Poddar interpreted this act as a sign of formal engagement (as it might have been in India, where he was a member of the Harijam or "untouchable caste"). [But] Tanya told him that she was involved with other men, and indicated that she did not wish to have an intimate relationship with him.

Poddar was depressed as a result of the rebuff, but he saw Tanya a few times during the spring (occasionally tape recording their conversations in an effort to understand why she did not love him). Tanya left for Brazil in the summer, and Poddar at the urging of a friend went to the student health facility where a psychiatrist referred him to a psychologist for psychotherapy. When Tanya returned in October 1969, Poddar discontinued therapy. Based in part on Poddar's stated intention to purchase a gun, the psychologist notified the campus police, both orally and in writing, that Poddar was dangerous and should be taken to a community mental health centre for psychiatric commitment.

The campus police interviewed Poddar, who seemed rational and promised to stay away from Tanya. They released him and notified the health service. No further efforts at commitment were made because the supervising psychiatrist apparently decided they were not needed and, as a matter of confidentiality, requested that the letter to the police and certain therapy records be destroyed.

On October 27, Poddar went to Tanya's home armed with a pellet gun and a kitchen knife. She refused to speak to him. He shot her with the pellet gun. She ran from the house, was pursued, caught, and repeatedly and fatally stabbed by him. Poddar was found guilty of voluntary manslaughter rather than first- or second-degree murder. The defence established

with the aid of the expert testimony of three psychiatrists that Poddar's diminished mental capacity, paranoid schizophrenia, precluded the malice necessary for first- or second-degree murder. After his prison term, he returned to India, where, according to his own report, he is happily married. (Schwitzgebel & Schwitzgebel, 1980, p. 205)

Under the privileged communication statute of California, the counselling centre psychologist properly breached the confidentiality of the professional relationship and took steps to have Poddar civilly committed, for he judged Poddar to be an imminent danger. Poddar had stated that he intended to purchase a gun, and he had convinced the therapist that he was desperate enough to harm Tarasoff. What the psychologist did not do, and what the court decided he should have done, was to warn the likely victim, Tarasoff, that her former friend had bought a gun and might use it against her. Such a warning would have been consistent with previous court decisions requiring physicians to warn the public when they are treating people with contagious diseases and requiring mental institutions to warn others when a dangerous patient has escaped (Knapp & Vandecreek, 1982). The Tarasoff ruling, now being applied in other states as well,[3] requires clinicians, in deciding when to violate confidentiality, to use the very imperfect skill of predicting dangerousness.

EXTENDING PROTECTION TO FORESEEABLE VICTIMS

A subsequent California court ruling[4] held, by a bare majority, that foreseeable victims include those in close relationship with the identifiable victim. In this instance, a mother was hurt by a shotgun fired by a dangerous patient, and her seven-year-old son was present when the shooting took place. The boy later sued the psychologists for damages brought on by emotional trauma. Since a young child is likely to be in the company of his or her mother, the court concluded in this case that the Tarasoff ruling extended to the boy.

CHILLING EFFECT OF TARASOFF?

In the years since the Tarasoff ruling, professionals have wondered whether it would have a negative effect, perhaps even a chilling effect, on psychotherapists. If clients are informed of this limitation to confidentiality, they may become reluctant to express feelings of extreme anger to therapists for fear that therapists will notify the people with whom they are angry. Clients might become less open with their therapists, perhaps derive less benefit from therapy, and even become more likely to inflict harm if they have not disclosed their fury as a first step toward controlling it. The welfare of the people whom the Tarasoff decision intended to protect might be endangered by the very ruling itself!

It is unclear whether these concerns are well-founded. A survey of psychologists and psychiatrists in California soon after Tarasoff became law indicated that the court decision was affecting their thinking and practices (Wise, 1978). On the plus side, one third reported consulting more often with colleagues concerning cases in which violence was an issue. This practice should have a good outcome, since input from other professionals may improve the solitary clinician's decision-making, presumably to the benefit of the client. (Consultation can also demonstrate that the clinician took extra steps to adhere to Tarasoff, which can reduce legal liability [Monahan, 1993].) On the minus side, about 20% of the respondents indicated that they avoided asking their clients questions about violence, an ostrich-like stance that may keep the clinician from obtaining important information and yet reduces his or her legal liability should the client harm someone. A substantial number of therapists were keeping less detailed records, again in an effort to reduce legal liability.

As for Canada, the courts have not established that it is the duty of psychologists to warn or protect others (see Heilbrun, Ogloff, and Picarello, 1999), but codes of ethics by professional organizations such as the Canadian Psychological Association stipulate clearly that psychologists must breach confidentiality when there is reason to suspect that a third party is at risk (see Ogloff, 1999). Thus, although confidentially typically prevails in the therapeutic setting, certain circumstances can lead the therapist to inform others of the possible dangers.

In a Tarasoff situation, the clinician is seeing a client in a counselling capacity and comes to suspect that third persons may be at risk. What about the forensic context? The Supreme Court of Canada has visited this issue with results that are as "chilling" as the civil context of Tarasoff. In Smith v. Jones (1999), Jones (an alias) had been charged with a number of sexual assaults on prostitutes in the Vancouver area. Counsel for the accused retained the services of a psychiatrist—Smith (also an alias)—to conduct a psychiatric assessment of his client. This is a routine procedure for defence counsel and is usually perceived to be risk-free, as the psychiatrist's assessment would be privileged in that he or she is acting in the capacity of counsel's agent or, alternatively, under the umbrella of the "solicitor-client brief." In Smith v. Jones, the psychiatrist, Smith, contacted counsel for the accused to inquire when the trial was to commence. Counsel advised Smith repeatedly that he would not be needed (in that his report was quite negative). Smith persisted, indicating that Jones was very dangerous and prospective victims should be warned. Counsel continued to rebuff Smith. Finally, Smith retained counsel and sought to intervene. The case went to the B.C. Trial Division, Court of Appeal, and finally to the Supreme Court of Canada, where it was held that, notwithstanding the privilege that would normally be expected in a situation of this sort, where a mental health professional is retained by counsel to perform an assessment and as a

Prosenjit Poddar was convicted of manslaughter in the death of Tatiana Tarasoff. The court ruled that his therapist, who had become convinced Poddar might harm Tarasoff, should have warned her of the impending danger.

result of that assessment the accused is seen as an imminent threat of serious bodily harm to an identifiable victim or class of victims, the clinician has an obligation to notify whomever, including the police, may be appropriate in the circumstances.

In this instance, Jones had outlined to Smith his detailed plans to kidnap and kill a small prostitute who could be physically overpowered. Jones planned to strangle the victim and dispose of her body in the bush near Hope, B.C. Jones had been diagnosed with multiple paraphilias, including sexual sadism, as well as drug abuse problems.

As a result of this decision, the defence bar is no longer able to rely upon the law of agency or the privilege that would attach to the gathering of information in anticipation of litigation—the solicitor-client brief. The frequency of referrals for assessments is anticipated to plummet, and ironically, it can be argued that the public safety concern driving the decision of the Supreme Court has actually been set back because now the prospectively dangerous accused will not be sent off for assessment by the defence bar unless the assessment is absolutely crucial. It is ironic because this is the clearest statement in Canada of a duty to warn and the decision is based on the principle that concerns about public safety outweigh the interest of doctor-patient confidentiality (Canadian Psychiatric Association, 2000). The Canadian Psychiatric Association (2004) responded to the case of Smith v. Jones by concluding that the position about the duty to warn taken by the Supreme Court of Canada is to be accepted as a professional standard of practice.

As an update to Tarasoff in California, in 2004, an appeals court ruled that a therapist has a duty to warn possible victims if the threat is reported to the therapist by a close member of the patient's family.[5]

[2] Tarasoff v. Regents of the University of California, 529 P.2d 553 (Cal. 1974), vacated, reheard in bank, and affirmed, 131 Cal. Rptr. 14, 551 P.2d 334 (1976). The 1976 California Supreme Court ruling was by a four-to-three majority.

[3] White v. United States, 780 F2D 97 (D.C. Cir. 1986); Soutear v. United States, 646 F.Supp. 524 (1986); Dunkle v. Food Services East Inc., 582 A.2d. 1342 (1990); People v. Clark, 50 Cal. 3d 583, 789 P.2d 127 (1990).

[4] Hedlund v. Superior Court, 34 Cal.3d 695 (1983).

[5] Ewing v. Goldstein, Cal. App.4th B163112.2d (2004).

TRENDS TOWARD GREATER PROTECTION

We turn now to a discussion of several issues and trends that revolve around the greater protections being provided to mental health patients in recent years: the right to treatment, the right to refuse treatment, and questions of free will in the law. We begin with a discussion of how to resolve complicated situations in which several themes may conflict in efforts to provide humane mental health treatment while respecting individual rights. Competing interests operate to create a complex and continually changing picture.

CHOOSING AMONG ETHICAL PRINCIPLES The ethical code prescribed by the American Psychological Association (APA) first appeared in 1953, and it was adopted and used for many years with minor changes by the Canadian Psychological Association and provincial associations (Sinclair, Poizner, Gilmour-Barrett, & Randall, 1987). One factor that provided the impetus for a separate code for Canadian psychologists was dissatisfaction with changes made to the APA code in 1979 (see Sinclair, 1993). Specifically, Canadian psychologists were concerned about a change that loosened restrictions on advertising by psychologists. As a result, work was undertaken on a Canadian code of ethics in the 1980s, leading in 1986 to the first Canadian Code of Ethics for Psychologists. The third edition of this code was published in 2000 (Canadian Psychological Association, 2000).

A particularly useful aspect of the Canadian ethics code is that it assists psychologists who must make decisions in situations where various ethics may be in conflict (Sinclair et al., 1987). Psychologists were surveyed about how they would respond to hypothetical scenarios, and the four most relevant principles were identified and rank-ordered by their importance. Following are the four principles:

1. *Respect for the dignity of persons*. This principle is given the most weight, especially when there is the possibility that anyone will be exposed to physical danger.
2. *Responsible caring*. This provision includes the notion that responsible caring occurs only when it is provided by competent individuals who are able to respect the dignity of other people.
3. *Integrity in relationships*. This principle applies to all relationships, but it is noted in the code of ethics that there may be times when a need to be open and candid with an individual may conflict with the need to respect the dignity of others, and if so, the emphasis is on respecting the dignity of others.
4. *Responsibility to society*. The ranking of this ethical principle as the fourth consideration in no way suggests that this is not an important guideline. Rather, the Canadian code emphasizes that when there is a conflict between the needs of the individual and the needs of society, the need to preserve the dignity of the individual should prevail.

The notion of responsibility to society is important because it stipulates that psychologists have a general duty to promote the welfare of human beings and enhance our society. This principle was seen as particularly important by Dobson, Dobson, and Ritchie (1993). In their call for involvement, they observed that

> sustained advocacy by professional psychology on a range of issues linking psychological knowledge, expertise and practice with the public good is both an ethical requirement, particularly from the perspective of social responsibility, as well as a matter of enlightened self-interest. Although there have been some examples of political advocacy, there are other areas in which psychology has been mute or passively acquiescent. The profession requires a system to derive clear and defensible social policy positions as well as the ability to act upon these positions. (p. 451)

The importance of this approach is certainly evident to the many psychology students in Canada who embrace similar values and become actively involved as volunteers in their local communities.

RIGHT TO TREATMENT An aspect of civil commitment that has received the attention of the courts is the so-called right to treatment, a principle first articulated by Birnbaum (1960). If a person is deprived of liberty because he or she is mentally ill and is a danger to self or others, is the state not required to provide treatment to alleviate these problems? Is it not unconstitutional (and even indecent) to incarcerate someone without then providing the required help? This key question has been the subject of several court cases since Birnbaum first articulated the issue.

In O'Connor v. Donaldson (1975), a celebrated case in the United States that eventually went to the Supreme Court, a civilly committed mental patient sued two state hospital doctors for his release and for monetary damages on the grounds that he had been incarcerated against his will for 14 years without being treated and without being dangerous to himself or to others. In January 1957, at the age of 49, Kenneth Donaldson had been committed to a Florida state hospital on petition of his father, who felt that his son was delusional. A county judge had found that Donaldson had paranoid schizophrenia and committed him for "care, maintenance, and treatment." The Florida statute then in effect allowed for such commitment on the usual grounds of mental illness and dangerousness, the latter defined as inability to manage property and to protect oneself from being taken advantage of by others.

In 1971, Donaldson sued Dr. O'Connor, the hospital superintendent, and Dr. Gumanis, a hospital psychiatrist, for release. Evidence presented at the trial indicated that the hospital staff could have released Donaldson at any time following a determination that he was not a dangerous person. Testimony made it clear that at no time during his hospitalization had Donaldson's conduct posed any real danger to others or to himself. The evidence indicated that Donaldson received only custodial care during his hospitalization. No treatment that could conceivably alleviate or cure his assumed mental illness was undertaken. The original trial and asubsequent appeal concluded that Donaldson was not dangerous and had been denied his constitutional right to treatment. Throughout this litigation, Donaldson declared that he was neither dangerous nor mentally ill. But, said his claim, even if he were mentally ill, he should be released because he was not receiving treatment. The U.S. Supreme Court ruled on June 26, 1975, that, "a State cannot constitutionally confine . . . a nondangerous individual who is capable of surviving safely in freedom by himself or with the help of willing and responsible family members or friends." In 1977, Donaldson settled for $20,000 from Dr. Gumanis and the estate of Dr. O'Connor, who died during the appeals process.

The Supreme Court decision on O'Connor v. Donaldson created a stir when it was issued and has since given mental health professionals pause in detaining patients. Although this decision is often cited as an affirmation of the right to treatment, the Supreme Court did not, in fact, rule on the constitutionality of this doctrine. The Donaldson decision did say that a committed patient's status must be periodically reviewed, for the grounds on which a patient was committed cannot be assumed to continue in effect forever. In other words, people can change while in a mental hospital and may no longer require confinement. This position seems straightforward enough, yet it may still be overlooked.

Presumably, a situation such as that found in Donaldson v. O'Connor would not occur in Canada since a precondition to civil commitment is a finding of danger to self or others, which is reviewed every 90 days or upon the patient's request.

RIGHT TO REFUSE TREATMENT If a committed patient has the right to expect appropriate treatment, does he or she have the right to refuse treatment or a particular kind of treatment? The answer is yes, depending on the province in question.

The case of Regina v. Rogers (1991; see Table 18.1) in British Columbia reiterated that mentally disordered individuals have the right to refuse treatment, even if they were civilly committed

against their personal wishes. Currently, the situation is more complicated when viewed from a national perspective. Douglas and Koch (2001) provided an up-to-date summary of how the right to refuse treatment varies from province to province. Some provinces maintain the patient's right to refuse treatment (e.g., Nova Scotia, Quebec, Ontario, and Manitoba), while others have provisions that allow for treatment without the individual's consent (e.g., Prince Edward Island, Newfoundland and Labrador, New Brunswick, and British Columbia). The situation is more complicated in Alberta, where mental health officials have the opportunity to apply to a review panel in order to override the patient's right to refuse treatment (Douglas & Koch, 2001). Typically, when the patient's right to refuse treatment is circumvented, a substitute decision-maker (i.e., family member) is asked to provide consent.

One alternative in provinces where a person can be given treatment without his or her consent is to have the person outline his or her wishes during a time when he or she was of sounder mind. According to Simmie and Nunes (2001), this concept is known as establishing a person's prior capable wish and this wish has been ruled valid in court cases in both Canada and the United States.

In Ontario, patients can only be treated against their will civilly where they are determined to be incapable of consent. In such cases, a scheme exists whereby substitute consent to treatment may be obtained. A potentially more interesting question arises around patients who do consent to treatment. Curiously, the issue of capacity to consent is rarely raised where the patient does consent to treatment. What percentage of those patients currently being treated "voluntarily" are actually incapable of consenting to their treatment?

In the case of Starson v. Swayze (2003), the Supreme Court of Canada confirmed the patient's right to refuse treatment. This case is the subject of Canadian Perspectives 18.2.

Opponents of the right to refuse treatment are concerned that mental hospitals will revert to being warehouses of

---

CANADIAN PERSPECTIVES 18.2

"A BEAUTIFUL MIND" IN CANADA? SCOTT STARSON AND THE RIGHT TO REFUSE TREATMENT

In some respects, Scott Starson is similar to John Nash, who was the subject of the book *A Beautiful Mind* by Sylvia Nasar and the subsequent Academy Award-winning movie starring Russell Crowe. Nash won a Nobel Prize in Economics for his contribution to game theory. He has a history of schizophrenia. Starson is a highly intelligent person with an abiding interest and expertise in physics as it pertains to the study of discrete anti-gravity and its implications for space travel.

Starson, who prefers to be referred to as Professor Starson, has authored some highly regarded articles in scientific journals despite not having any formal training in physics and not being an actual professor. Starson suffers from schizoaffective disorder, a condition that combines symptoms of schizophrenia and bipolar disorder. In 1998,

he was found not criminally responsible on account of mental disorder after uttering death threats. Specifically, he phoned his work colleagues and informed them that he was in a phone booth with a rifle and was going to shoot the sales manager of a car dealership where he had been turned down for a lease or loan (Wente, 2003). He also threatened to kill his psychiatrist (Bailey, 2002).

Starson is an involuntary psychiatric patient who has been detained in psychiatric hospitals in Penetanguishene and Ottawa and has experienced mental difficulties since 1985. There is no doubt that he suffers from mental illness. According to one interview account, he indicated that "Pope John Paul II works for me now." He also indicated that he had plans to wed comedian Joan Rivers, though he had never met her. He also believes that former

Scott Starson is a physics savant.

Prime Minister Pierre Elliott Trudeau was killed by an alien (see Bailey, 2003).

Starson gained notoriety for successfully winning a legal case in which his right to refuse treatment was upheld by the Supreme Court of Canada in a six to three decision. He argued that the drug medication was ineffective and would take away his mental faculties. In his statement to the Court of Appeal for Ontario, he observed:

> Well, like all psychiatrists that I've met before them, they all think the same way, that the only thing they can do is to give you these chemicals—and I've been through these chemicals that they propose before—and I know the effects and what they want to achieve is slow down my brain, basically, and to slow down my brain which means I can't do what I've been trying to do—or what I have been doing for 30 years and will be successful at doing. And that would just be like worse than death.

In its ruling, the Supreme Court supported the ruling of two previous courts that had overturned the initial ruling of the Ontario Consent and Capacity Board (CCB), which ruled that Starson did not have the right to refuse treatment. The Supreme Court based its decision on the observation that the Ontario CCB based its initial ruling on what the board felt was in the best treatment interests of Starson rather than on a strict interpretation of his legal rights (see Brooks, O'Reilly, & Gray, 2003). It is still the case that patients have the right to refuse treatment if they are deemed to be capable of making this decision, but if it can be shown that they are incapacitated based on "a balance of probabilities," then treatment can be forced on them (Brooks et al., 2003).

Regardless of whether one agrees with the Supreme Court decision, it is hard not to feel sorry for Starson's mother, Jeanne Stevens. According to Bailey (2003), she wants her son to receive treatment and, in reaction to the court decision, she stated, "I'm devastated. I don't think what they did was a humane judgement. It's a disaster because they have destroyed his life and his dream."

Starson does acknowledge that he has mental problems, but he notes that he distrusts psychiatry, which he views as a religion. A year after winning the right to refuse treatment, Starson almost died. He became delusional and refused all offers of food and water due to his fear of being poisoned. According to a Canadian Press article (2006), Starson was granted a transfer to Toronto after finally agreeing to take his medication.

By the way, Starson's original surname is Schutzman. According to his mother, he changed it in 1993 because "he actually thought he was the son of the stars."

THINKING CRITICALLY

1. Do you agree or disagree with the Supreme Court decision? Should Starson have the right to refuse treatment?

2. The decision was based on a strict interpretation of Starson's legal rights. What about the feelings and wishes of Starson's mother? Does she have any right to support forced treatment? Was the court's decision inhumane?

3. Are there any circumstances when it is in society's best interests for a person to be treated against his or her will?

poorly treated patients. Psychiatrists fear that lawyers and judges will not accept that some people are too mentally ill to be believed, or too mentally disturbed to be able to make sound judgements about their treatment. In a book on what he calls America's mental health crisis, psychiatrist E. Fuller Torrey asserts that upwards of 90% of psychotic patients have no insight into their condition. Believing that they do not need any treatment, they subject themselves and loved ones to sometimes desperate and frightening situations by refusing medication or other modes of therapy, most of which involve hospitalization (Torrey, 1996).

DEINSTITUTIONALIZATION, CIVIL LIBERTIES, AND MENTAL HEALTH

Since the 1960s, provinces throughout Canada have embarked on a policy of deinstitutionalization, discharging as many patients as possible from mental hospitals and discouraging admissions. The maxim is now "Treat them in the community," the assumption being that virtually anything is preferable to institutionalization.

Barnes and Toews (1983) assessed deinstitutionalization in Canada and concluded that it had occurred at the same rate in Canada as in the United States. They cited a 1974 study that indicated that there was a 43% reduction in the number of patients in public mental institutions between 1960 and 1972, as well as a 1979 Statistics Canada report showing a decrease by 50% of beds in institutions. Barnes and Toews also noted that patients fare no worse in the community than in an institution, with the vital provision that this depended substantially on the quality of care and provisions for care made available when people were released to the community. Research studies on care in the hospital vs. care in the home in Montreal (e.g., Fenton, Tessier, & Streuning, 1979) and in Vancouver (Goodacre et al., 1975) yielded few differences. Other research suggests that the quality of life can even be significantly better in the community (Lord & Pedlar, 1991), but Canadian investigators continue to emphasize that the quality and availability of aftercare is a vital consideration (e.g., Lesage & Morissette, 1993). Ideally, most discharged people will get into highly supervised settings, as was shown to be the case in a study conducted in Quebec. Lesage et al. (2000) found that long-stay patients released from Canada's largest psychiatric hospital (i.e., the Louis-H Lafontaine Hospital) were not abandoned.

Deinstitutionalization is a phenomenon that has taken place across Canada. Simmie and Nunes (2001) observed:

> New Brunswick recently demolished its oldest psychiatric hospital, and former residents are now doing well in the community. Many of these people have spent years, even decades, on the inside. "I never thought that some of the people coming out would make it," says the director of a community mental health centre in Fredericton, "but in fact their needs have declined." (p. 162)

But what is this community that former mental hospital patients are supposed to find more helpful to them on discharge? Facilities outside hospitals are often not prepared to cope with the influx of these patients. Some promising programs were described in Chapter 11, but these are very much the exception, not the rule. The state of affairs in many large metropolitan areas is an unrelenting social crisis, for hundreds of thousands of chronically ill mental health patients across North America were released without sufficient job training and without community services to help them. It is doubtful, too, that deinstitutionalization reduced the rate of chronic mental illness. As Gralnick (1987) argued, acutely ill persons are largely neglected because it is difficult to commit them unless they are found to be a danger to themselves and others, a state that can take years to develop; by that time, their problems may have become chronic and more difficult to deal with. The irony is that deinstitutionalization may be contributing to the very problem it was designed to alleviate, chronic mental illness.

Indeed, deinstitutionalization may be a misnomer. *Transinstitutionalization* may be more apt, for declines in the census of public mental hospitals have occasioned increases in the numbers of mentally ill people in jails, prisons, nursing homes, and the mental health departments of non-psychiatric hospitals (e.g., Cloud, 1999), and these settings are often not equipped to handle the particular needs of mental health patients. The oft-mentioned revolving door was seen in the increase in readmission rates, from 25% before the deinstitutionalization movement to around 80% by the 1980s (Paul & Menditto, 1992).

In late 2004, Ontario Superior Court Justice Robert Desmarais (see Rupert, 2005), in a landmark ruling intended to be binding on all Ontario courts, ruled there was no legal authority to jail mentally ill people pending in-custody forensic assessments and indicated that jailing them violated their

Charter of Rights guarantees not to be arbitrarily detained. Although the Ontario health ministry announced an infusion of money to deal with these individuals, the government had not increased the beds within the six-month period ordered by the judge. Health Minister George Smitherman had admitted that there had been a 27% increase in the number of mentally ill people incarcerated in correctional facilities in Ontario between 1995 and 2005. Subsequently, The Right Honourable Beverley McLachlin, as Chief Justice of the Supreme Court of Canada, lamented the fact that the courts and judges are facing a crisis because community-based care has never been properly funded (see Bailey & Bronskill, 2006). The Chief Justice was encouraged by steps such as mental health courts in Ontario and New Brunswick designed to divert the mentally ill from jail into treatment programs. However, Justice Richard Schneider, who presides over Canada's first mental health court at Old City Hall in Toronto, has stated that the government needs to involve fewer mentally ill people in the criminal justice system or provide more beds for assessment and treatment (*Toronto Star*, 2005). The mentally ill are ending up in the criminal courts in unprecedented numbers. Schneider (2000) previously reported that across Canada the number of mentally disordered accused coming before provincial review boards has been increasing at a minimum of 10% per year since the early 1990s, while overall prosecution rates have been decreasing. It may be naive to expect that the community from which the mentally disordered individual came is the one best suited to provide support and treatment.

Many patients discharged from mental hospitals are eligible for social benefits, but a large number are not receiving this assistance. Financial and occupational concerns are very salient. A qualitative study examined the deinstitutionalization experience and the issues that faced 139 people who were previously institutionalized in Eastern Canada (Herman & Smith, 1989). Six significant themes emerged: (1) stigmatization of people with a history of mental illness; (2) an

The Honourable Mr. Justice Richard Schneider, the judge at Canada's first mental health court in Toronto, is also trained as a clinical psychologist. He is a tireless advocate for the psychiatric assessment and treatment of mentally ill people who come before the courts.

absence of basic living skills; (3) poor housing; (4) poverty; (5) difficulties getting a job; and (6) difficulties accessing after-care programs.

Homeless persons do not have fixed addresses and need help in establishing eligibility and residency for the purpose of receiving benefits. Nowadays, especially in larger cities, it is common to see people who have been discharged from psychiatric hospitals living in the streets, in train and bus terminals, in abandoned buildings, on subways, and in shelters operated by public agencies, churches, and charitable organizations. In Toronto alone, there are about 25,000 such people (Goering et al., 2000), and comparable situations exist in other major cities throughout Canada. The lives of these individuals are desperate.

Discharged mental health patients who are not homeless may live marginal lives in nursing homes, jails, and rundown hotels. Although a visible part of the population, their visibility may be diminishing, as many other people have been dispossessed from their homes and have lost their jobs. The state of homelessness exacerbates the emotional suffering of former mental health patients. Mentally ill peolpe are an especially defenceless segment of the homeless population.

The links between homelessness and mental illness have been extensively documented. A study of homelessness in Toronto found that approximately two thirds of the 300 people assessed had lifetime diagnoses of mental illness (Tolomiczenko & Goering, 1998). Moreover, two thirds of the participants had some form of substance abuse. Stuart and Arboleda-Florez (2000) assessed homeless shelter users in Calgary and found that approximately one third had a significant mental health problem and that the lifetime prevalence of alcohol abuse was 33.6%. Greater psychiatric problems were associated with a wider range of hardships, health risks, victimization, negative life events (including economic problems), and a sense of dissatisfaction. Acorn (1993) surveyed users of an emergency shelter in British Columbia and found that depression, anxiety, and tension were quite common; approximately one fifth of the respondents acknowledged a current mental disorder, with schizophrenia and bipolar disorder being most evident. Another investigation of jail detainees confirmed links between homelessness and severe mental disorder, as well as prior psychiatric

history (Zapf, Roesch, & Hart, 1996). Such problems are probably aggravated by a nomadic and dangerous existence. Homeless people, especially women, are likely victims of violence and rape, even when living in shelters for the homeless (D'Ercole & Struening, 1990). Children are also found among the homeless population. These youngsters are forced to live their formative years in chaotic and dangerous situations, with parents under severe stress. It comes as no surprise that these children are often subjected to abuse and many drop out of school and suffer from anxiety, depression, and substance abuse.

Do such appalling conditions, still found today, justify reversing the policy of deinstitutionalization? In our view, no, because the problem lies with the failure of communities to provide suitable living and rehabilitation conditions, an issue discussed earlier in this book. There are, however, signs that the pendulum may begin to swing back in the direction of more involuntary hospitalization, even when the person does not pose a real danger to his- or herself or to others but is wandering homeless on the streets and living in squalor. Being "persistently and acutely disabled" is, in some United States jurisdictions, replacing "being a danger to oneself or to others" (Shogren, 1994). It remains to be seen how this trend will develop in light of laws and court rulings that have been making it more and more difficult to keep people institutionalized against their will. In an interesting twist, it was reported recently (Fong, 2007) that the Mayor of Vancouver wants to re-institutionalize some former residents of Riverview Hospital in suburban Coquitlam who ended up in Vancouver's Downtown Eastside where housing is generally unavailable and drugs are readily available. It is estimated that about 40% of the homeless people in B.C.'s Lower Mainland are mentally ill. Riverview once held about 5,000 patients but as a result of deinstitutionalization the number dwindled to about 400 people. The mayor has proposed new modern spaces that provide support rather than a return to old-style locked wards.

Some people fear that individuals with schizophrenia are increasingly being seen as misfits, drug abusers, and panhandlers rather than as ill people in need of professional care. Canadian Perspectives 18.3 describes some recommended solutions to the problems of deinstitutionalization in Canada.

CANADIAN PERSPECTIVES 18.3
SOLUTIONS TO THE CONSEQUENCES OF DEINSTITUTIONALIZATION IN CANADA

"Whether it's a friend, a colleague or someone living in a bus shelter, there are really only eight kinds of people affected by mental health problems: Someone's mother, daughter, sister or wife; someone's father, husband, brother or son. People. Like me"

—Scott Simmie, October 10, 1998, author of the "Atkinson Fellowship investigation into mental health," published as the eight-part "Out of Mind" series in the *Toronto Star* (October 3–10, 1998). Simmie has suffered from bipolar disorder.

In the spring of 1998, two investigative reporters for the *Toronto Star*, Donovan Vincent and Theresa Boyle, wrote a seven-part series (entitled "Madness") that was based on their investigations of the human tragedy of mental illness. Later, in the fall of 1998, Scott Simmie, winner of the Atkinson Fellowship in Public Policy, wrote an eight-part *Toronto Star* series (entitled "Out of Mind") that was based on his year-long exploration of mental health reform. Both series of articles concluded with long lists of recommendations and steps that should be taken for the benefit of

Scott Simmie, author of the "Out of Mind" series about the plight of the mentally ill. His investigations led to many proposed and implemented solutions to the consequences of deinstitutionalization.

people with serious and chronic mental illness. In our opinion, these series covered the issues in a constructive, responsible, and fair way.

In an assessment of the Simmie series, Goering et al. (2000) stated:

> The combination of personal account and careful investigative reporting created a powerful series that was educational, destigmatizing, and much appreciated by mental health consumers and providers. Unfortunately, such coverage of mental health by the Canadian press is the exception, not the rule.

In the final segment of his own series, Simmie prefaced his proposed solutions in a poignant way:

> Today is World Mental Health Day. Its theme: human rights and mental health. As a country, we love to talk about human rights and point an admonishing finger abroad when we see things we don't like. It's time we looked closer to home. We are abusing the human rights of many of our citizens. People stricken with serious and chronic mental health problems. We marginalize them in every way. We abandon them as friends, avoid them on the street. And we provide them with income supports that keep them in second-hand clothes—at best. But our greatest shame is our failure to supply the most fundamental need of any human being. A home. That's where true mental health reform must begin. . . . Drugs are critical for schizophrenia—but the best medication means nothing if your home is a bus shelter. (Simmie, 1998, October 10.)

STEPS TO TAKE

Boyle and Vincent (1998) and Simmie (1998) listed steps that must be taken in Ontario to help people with serious and chronic mental health problems. Most of their recommendations can be applied right across Canada. Throughout this section, we use the preferred term for current and former psychiatric patients, as determined by the patients and former patients themselves: "consumers/survivors." Consistent with the changes associated with the "new CAMH" described in Chapter 11, we also accept the term "client" as a preferred term. The following is an integrated list of the steps, plus some additional recommendations:

- Reinvestment of funds (approximately $400 million in 1998) into community mental health services (such as crisis centres, crisis lines, and child and adolescent programs). In particular, there is a need for 80 assertive-community response teams. This reinvestment would not only be humane, there would be substantial cost savings coupled with a reduction of disability and mortality.

- Review and changes to the *Mental Health Act* consistent with change from the old and outdated "institutional model" to a "community-oriented system" model.

- A variety of supportive housing, ranging from independent apartments to group homes, coupled with monitoring of standards and maintenance, particularly for boarding homes and rooming houses. At least 14,000 units are needed.

- An expanded home care program for people with serious mental disorders. (This recommendation is, of course, consistent with the recommendation of the Romanow Report and Kirby Report summarized in Chapter 1.)

- Community mental health centres as standard access points to the mental health "system" where people can receive assistance on site and appropriate referrals. Consumer/survivor advocates would be a part of multidisciplinary teams.

- Incentives to adequately staff provincial psychiatric hospitals (professional as well as support staff), especially those slated for closure.

- Development, evaluation, and implementation of risk assessment tools for forensic patients to facilitate the best use of resources and bed space.

- Opening of additional forensic beds for mentally ill offenders, to eliminate the problem of the mentally ill being incarcerated in jails.

- Diversion of the mentally ill from the criminal justice system if possible, as well as the hiring of additional mental health workers in jails.

- Community treatment orders should be a last resort.

- The most effective (but sometimes most expensive) medications for schizophrenia should be available as "first-line" treatment.

- Increased emphasis on early detection and treatment of mental disorders in children. Emphasis on "defragmenting" children's services should have high priority.

- More non-medical safe houses for people in crisis, patterned after Toronto's Gerstein Centre.

- Government-established 24-hour information/crisis lines staffed by consumers/survivors who are trained to refer people to appropriate resources.

- Expansion of consumer/survivor alternative businesses to provide work and "restore dignity and hope" to former psychiatric patients (survivors). For example, the Ontario Council of Alternative Businesses helps consumers/survivors initiate and operate businesses, such as A-Way Express, a courier service. Fresh Start, another example, is a cleaning and maintenance company staffed and run by psychiatric survivors.

- Expanded income supports and reduction of penalties for consumers/survivors who attempt to supplement their income. (In 1998, typical monthly benefits under the Ontario Disability Support Program were about $700 per month.)

- Extension or subsidizing of drug benefits under the Ontario Drug Benefits Program for consumers/survivors who want to fully rejoin the workforce.

- Development of alternative payment schemes that will encourage psychiatrists to treat people with severe, persistent mental illnesses. Awareness by psychiatrists of, and referral to where appropriate, all the services and resources in their local community. General practitioners (usually the initial point of contact) should consult actively with psychiatrists.

- Support for anti-stigma campaigns by the Ministry of Health or Health Canada, in consultation with the Canadian Mental Health Association.

- Encouragement of co-operation among community service providers. (Such co-operation should not be legislated.)

- Support on the part of employers for employees with mental health problems.

- Encouraging the mentally ill to seek help from each other through various associations (such as the local chapter of the Mood Disorders Association).

- Increased training for the police in ways to deal with the mentally ill, including alternative "use of force" strategies to prevent the deaths of psychotic individuals.

- Appropriate contextual statements in all news stories linking violence and mental illness, since the seriously mentally ill are responsible for only 4% of the violence in society.

- A decision on how a reformed mental health system should be managed. As noted by Boyle and Vincent, as of 1998, in Ontario, there were 10 provincial hospitals (e.g., Queen Street Mental Health Centre in Toronto), 65 general hospital psychiatric units, four specialty psychiatric hospitals, and more than 300 community mental health and addiction programs. They summarized the system as follows: "It's an uncoordinated patchwork of services with too few bridges between them and too many mentally ill falling through the cracks" (p. F4). Simmie recommended that the Government of Ontario create a "mental health commission" with a mandate to create a mental health "system," adequate

transitional funding, and authority to fund and build supportive housing.

- The public must re-examine their views of mental illness, help to reduce stigma, and lobby politicians to instigate changes.

Sources: This section was adapted primarily from Boyle and Vincent (1998) and Simmie (1998).

CHANGES?

These two series of carefully researched, thoughtful, provocative, and timely articles on mental health garnered tremendous public support and sympathy for consumers/survivors. They compelled various levels of government to begin to make many of the proposed changes, at least as pilot projects, and forced an ongoing consideration and evaluation of other options. The following are some of the positive changes that are already affecting the treatment of serious and chronic mental illness in our society:

- The creation of the restructured and integrated Centre for Addiction and Mental Health

- Diversion of the mentally ill from jails through the establishment of special courts and judges with special training (Ontario Court of Justice mental health court)

- Expansion of the assertive-response team program

- Expanded training of the police, such as the creation of special teams that include social workers riding in the patrol cars

- Creation of additional forensic beds in Toronto

- Input on the part of stakeholders, including consumers/survivors, into the final legislation creating community treatment orders

- Creation of anti-stigma campaigns

- Additional government funding targeted to community supports

- Promises of funding for supportive housing

There is obviously a long way to go toward full implementation of the proposed steps, not only in Ontario but throughout Canada. It is clear from Simmie's series that he considers supportive housing to be a critical step, and a number of initiatives have been taken in this area. However, progress has been slow. A year after the Ontario government had committed $100 million to fight homelessness, only about $30 million had been spent (Brennan, 2000). About half the money designated for the homeless mentally ill ($45 million) had been paid out to community organizations in Toronto, Hamilton, and Ottawa.

Of course, provinces can also learn from each other's strategies and efforts, and Ontario is not the only province facing significant challenges. The B.C. Early Intervention Study (see Macnaughton, 1998) was a survey conducted by the B.C. chapter of the CMHA to evaluate people's first experiences with the mental health system. This report documented, among other things, the length of time for people to get treatment. According to Macnaughton (1998), it took three years on average from first onset for people with schizophrenia and schizoaffective disorder to access treatment, and it took one year to access care from the time of acute onset. It took seven to eight years on average from first onset for people with mood disorders to access care, and it took six months to access care from the time of acute onset. A related problem that undermined treatment was that almost half of the survey's participants received an incorrect diagnosis during the early years of treatment. The most common misdiagnoses were interpreting bipolar disorder and early psychosis as depression and failing to make dual diagnoses involving various mental illnesses in combination with substance abuse. Community-based crisis response systems may not address the misdiagnosis issue but could perhaps result in quicker care.

Concerns about access to psychological services have also been raised in Alberta. The Alberta Alliance on Mental Illness and Mental Health (a coalition that includes the Psychologists' Association of Alberta) issued a call in March 2000 for the Alberta government to implement a comprehensive community care strategy. This group expressed concern about rates of suicide in Alberta and outlined a strategy with four components to address this problem (see http://www.psychologistsassociation.ab.ca):

- continuing efforts to promote public awareness of suicide as a preventable, public health problem

- eliminating barriers in public and private insurance programs and establishing incentives for treating people with coexisting mental illness and substance-abuse disorders

- increasing the use of schools and workplaces as access and referral points for services

- increasing research on risk and protective factors, as well as prevention programs, psychological treatment for suicidal individuals, and culture-specific interventions

In October 2003, this same group reiterated that all Albertans should have equal and timely access to mental health services (see Position Paper Regarding the Future of Mental Health Services in Alberta).

According to Goering et al. (2000), community-based crisis response systems (connected interventions that range from least to most intrusive) are most well developed in the province of Manitoba. In Manitoba, most regions rely heavily on "mobile crisis teams" as well as on "free-standing crisis centres" in support of people with serious and chronic mental health problems.

As noted in Chapter 1, there is also a shortage of mental health professionals in many regions of Canada. For example, the Canadian Psychiatric Association recommends one psychiatrist for every 8,400 citizens. In 2005, in the region of Peel, in the Greater Toronto Area, with a population of 1.5 million, there were only 54 psychiatrists instead of the recommended 130 (see Ogilvie, 2007). Although there should be 30 child psychiatrists for the region's 300,000 children, it's estimated that there are fewer than 10. Toronto currently has 500 more psychiatrists than the recommended ratio. In its 2007 annual Report on Ontario's Health System, the Ontario Health Quality Council (2007) discussed the shortage of health care professionals in Ontario and described mental health as one of the most severely under-resourced areas of health care.

THINKING CRITICALLY

1. Some recommendations in this section have already been implemented, but the majority have not. Review the proposed steps and choose the five recommendations that you consider to be most critical. Explain why you chose them. Outline a plan for implementing your recommendations.

2. What steps do you believe will be most difficult to gain acceptance for—from politicians, practitioners, and possibly the consumers/survivors themselves?

3. What would you do to increase the number of qualified mental health practitioners in under-serviced regions of Canada?

ETHICAL DILEMMAS IN THERAPY AND RESEARCH

In this textbook, we have examined a variety of theories and a multitude of data that focus on what is and what is thought to be. Ethics and values, often embodied in laws, are a different order of discussion. They concern what ought to be, having sometimes little to do with what is. It is extremely important to recognize the difference.

Within a given scientific paradigm, we are able to examine what we believe is reality. As the study of philosophy and ethics reveals, however, the statements people have made for thousands of years about what should be are another matter. The Ten Commandments are such statements. They are prescriptions and proscriptions about human conduct.

The legal trends reviewed thus far place limits on the activities of mental health professionals. These legal constraints are important, for laws are one of society's strongest means of encouraging all of us to behave in certain ways. Mental

health professionals also have professional and ethical constraints. All professional groups promulgate "shoulds" and "should nots," and by guidelines and mandates, they limit to some degree what therapists and researchers should do with their patients, clients, and research participants. Courts, too, have ruled on some of these questions. Most of the time what we believe is unethical is also illegal, but sometimes existing laws are in conflict with our moral sense of right and wrong. We examine now the ethics of making psychological inquiries and interventions into the lives of other human beings.

ETHICAL RESTRAINTS ON RESEARCH

Basic to the nature of science is the saying "What can be done will usually be attempted." The most reprehensible ethical insensitivity was evidenced in the brutal experiments conducted by German physicians on concentration camp prisoners during the Second World War. One experiment, for example, investigated how long people lived when their heads

The Nuremberg trials

were bashed repeatedly with a heavy stick. Even if important information might be obtained from this kind of experiment, such actions violate our sense of decency and morality. The Nuremberg Trials, conducted by the Allies following the war, brought these experiments and other barbarisms to light and meted out severe punishment to some of the soldiers, physicians, and Nazi officials who had engaged in or contributed to such actions, even when they claimed that they had merely been following orders. It would be reassuring to be able to say that such gross violations of human decency take place only during incredible and cruel epochs, such as the Third Reich, but unfortunately, this is not the case. Spurred on by a blind enthusiasm for their work, researchers have sometimes dealt with human subjects in reproachable ways.

Henry K. Beecher, a research professor at Harvard Medical School, surveyed medical research from 1946 to 1965 and found that "many of the patients [used as subjects in experiments] never had the risk satisfactorily explained to them, and . . .further hundreds have not known that they were the subjects of an experiment although grave consequences have been suffered as the direct result" (1966, p. 1354). Half a century later, in January 1994, spurred on by Eileen Welsome, a journalist who won a Pulitzer Prize for her investigative reporting on the issue, the U.S. Energy Department began to publicize numerous experiments conducted in the 1950s through the 1970s that had exposed hundreds of people— usually without their informed consent or prior knowledge— to harmful doses of radiation. There was particular concern over the fact that the overwhelming majority were people of low socio-economic status, members of racial minorities, people with mental retardation, nursing home patients, or prisoners. The scientists, for the most part supported in their research with federal funds, clearly understood that the risks were great, even though relatively little was known about the harmful effects of radiation at the time, for, as was pointed out by a lawyer arguing for compensation for some of the subjects, "they were doing it to poor and black people. You didn't see them doing it at the Mayo Clinic" (as quoted in Healy, 1994). Some of these experiments involved giving women in the third trimester of pregnancy a radioactive tonic to determine safe levels of exposure and irradiating the testicles of

prisoners to find out the degree of radiation that service personnel could endure without negative effects on sperm production. It is particularly troubling that these studies took place many years after the Nuremberg Trials.

The training of scientists equips them splendidly to pose interesting questions, sometimes even important ones, and to design research that is as free as possible of confounding elements. They have no special qualifications, however, for deciding whether a particular line of inquiry that involves humankind should be followed. Society needs knowledge, and a scientist has a right in a democracy to seek that knowledge. However, the ordinary citizens employed as participants in experiments must be protected from harm, risk, humiliation, and invasion of privacy.

Several international codes of ethics pertain to the conduct of scientific research: the Nuremberg Code formulated in 1947 in the aftermath of the Nazi war-crime trials, the 1964 Declaration of Helsinki, and statements from the British Medical Research Council. As for Canada, Young (1998) noted that medical research (including psychiatric investigations) in Canada is governed by four documents: the Nuremberg Code, the Declaration of Helsinki, the Medical Research Council of Canada's document *Guidelines on Research Involving Human Subjects* (1987), and the Tri-Council Working Group on Ethics (1998) document *Ethical Conduct for Research Involving Humans* (final report). The three councils that compose the Tri-Council Working Group are the Medical Research Council of Canada (MRC), the Natural Sciences and Engineering Research Council of Canada (NSERC), and the Social Sciences and Humanities Research Council of Canada (SSHRC).

In 1974, the U.S. Department of Health, Education, and Welfare began to issue guidelines and regulations governing scientific research that employs human and animal subjects. In addition, a blue-ribbon panel, the National Commission for the Protection of Human Subjects of Biomedical and Behavioral Research, issued a report in 1978 that arose from hearings and inquiries into restrictions that the U.S. government might impose on research performed with prisoners, children, and patients in psychiatric institutions. These various codes and principles are continually being re-evaluated and revised as new challenges are posed to the research community.

For the past 30 years, the proposals of behavioural researchers, many of whom conduct experiments related to psychopathology and therapy, have been reviewed for safety and general ethical propriety by institutional review boards in hospitals, universities, and research institutes. Such committees—and this is significant—comprise not only behavioural scientists but also citizens from the community, lawyers, students, and specialists in a variety of disciplines, such as professors of English, history, and comparative religion. They are able to block any research proposal or require questionable aspects to be modified if, in their collective judgement, the research would put participants at too great a risk. Such committees also now pass judgement on the scientific merits of proposals, the rationale being that it is not ethical to recruit participants for studies that will not yield valid data (e.g., Capron, 1999).

Changes in the Declaration of Helsinki are being debated, spurred on by two developments in biomedical research. The first is an increase in research sponsored by for-profit organizations such as pharmaceutical companies. Faced with fierce competition and marketplace pressures to maximize profits, such companies may push for research that would not be approved by human subjects committees in non-profit organizations such as universities. This issue came to a head when the International Committee of Medical Journal Editors (ICMJE), a group that includes the *Canadian Medical Association Journal* (CMAJ), issued an extensive set of rules and new policies that will govern the publication of results in major journals (see CMAJ, 2001). A CMAJ editorial on this issue stated:

> Henceforth, these 11 leading journals will require authors to attest that they "had full access to all of the data in [the] study and . . . [would] take complete responsibility for the integrity of the data and the accuracy of the data analysis." In addition, editors will retain the right to review the study protocol as well as funding contracts for the study before accepting the paper for publication. CMAJ will not accept reports on research that was conducted under a contractual arrangement that did not meet these ethical standards. (CMAJ, 2001, p. 733)

This position was reached in response to concerns that results could have been altered or even suppressed if the findings did not yield the results anticipated by the funding body.

The internationalization of research is a second factor in the possible attenuation of protection of human subjects. Developing countries are particularly eager for partnerships in research and do not always have the same historical commitment to individual informed consent and safety that is prevalent in more industrialized and democratic countries. A possible danger is that utilitarian standards (e.g., will the research yield generally useful results?) are becoming more important than the focus of the past half-century on the rights and safety of individual research participants.

In reaction to some ethical lapses in hospital-based research with mental health patients, the National Bioethics Advisory Commission recommends special precautions to ensure that research subjects with mental illness fully understand the risks and benefits of any research they are asked to participate in and that particular care be taken to make certain that they can decline or withdraw from research without feeling coerced. Specifically, instead of simply allowing a guardian or family member to make the decision for the patient, the commission proposes that a health professional who has nothing to do with the particular study make a judgement on whether a given patient can give informed consent. The commission recommends also that if a guardian is allowed to give consent on behalf of a patient judged incompetent to do so, then the guardian's own ability to give consent must be evaluated (Capron, 1999).

INFORMED CONSENT

This concern about conducting research with mental health patients underscores the all-important concept of informed consent. Just as committed mental health patients are gaining some right to refuse treatment, so may anyone refuse to be a participant in an experiment. The investigator must provide enough information to enable people to judge whether they want to accept any risks inherent in being a participant. Prospective participants must be legally capable of giving consent, and there must be no deceit or coercion in obtaining it. Furthermore, those who begin to participate as research subjects are free to withdraw at any time without fear of penalty.

Much research is relatively innocuous, but what if the experiment poses real risks, such as ingesting a drug, or what if a patient with schizophrenia whose condition has improved by taking a drug is withdrawn from it so that the investigator can assess the effects of "drug washout"? Or what if the prospective participant is a committed mental patient, or a child with mental retardation, unable to understand fully what is being asked? Such a person may not feel free or even be able to refuse participation. Although research shows that even committed patients with schizophrenia may be competent to understand and participate in treatment decisions, the degree of coercion that is part and parcel of being in a hospital setting must not be overlooked.

A further complication is that it is not always easy to demonstrate that a researcher has obtained informed consent. In an elaborate study, Stuart (1978) discovered that most college students could not accurately describe a simple experiment, even though it had just been explained to them and they had agreed to participate. A signature on a consent form is no assurance that informed consent has been obtained, which poses a challenge to investigators and members of review panels who are committed to upholding codes of ethics governing participation of human subjects in research.

Such problems are especially pronounced in clinical settings where patients may or may not understand the nature of antipsychotic medication. Irwin et al. (1985) found that although most patients said they understood the benefits and side effects of their drugs, only a quarter of them could actually demonstrate such understanding when queried specifically. Simply reading information to hospitalized patients—especially the more disturbed ones—is no guarantee that they fully comprehend; therefore, informed consent may not have been obtained. The report of the National Bioethics Advisory Commission pointed to many published experiments involving mental health patients in which no effort was made to determine whether the research participants had the decision-making capacity to give informed consent (Capron, 1999).

Still, as with the right to refuse treatment, there is recognition that being judged mentally ill—more specifically, being diagnosed with schizophrenia and being hospitalized—does not necessarily mean being incapable of giving informed consent. An experiment by Grisso and Applebaum (1991) found that although patients with schizophrenia on average understood issues relating to treatment involving medication less well than non-psychiatric patients did, there was a wide range of understanding among the patients; in fact, the understanding of some was as good as that of non-psychiatric patients. These results suggest that it is important to examine each person individually for ability to give informed consent, rather than assume that a person is unable to do so by virtue of being hospitalized.

CONFIDENTIALITY AND PRIVILEGED COMMUNICATION

When an individual consults a physician, psychiatrist, or clinical psychologist, he or she is assured by professional ethics codes that what goes on in the session will remain confidential. Confidentiality means that nothing will be revealed to a third party, except to other professionals and those intimately involved in the treatment, such as a nurse or medical secretary.

A privileged communication goes even further. It is communication between parties in a confidential relationship that is protected by law. The recipient of such a communication cannot legally be compelled to disclose it as a witness. The right of privileged communication is a major exception to the access courts have to evidence in judicial proceedings. Society believes that in the long term the interests of people are best served if communications to a spouse and to certain professionals remain off limits to the prying eyes and ears of the police, judges, and prosecutors. The privilege applies to such relationships as those between husband and wife, physician and patient, pastor and penitent, attorney and client, and psychologist and patient. The legal expression is that the patient or client "holds the privilege," which means that only he or she may release the other person to disclose confidential information in a legal proceeding.

There are important limits to a client's right of privileged communication, however. For example, according to the current California psychology licensing law (similar elements are present in other state and provincial laws), this right is eliminated for any of the following reasons:

- The client has accused the therapist of malpractice. In such a case, the therapist can divulge information about the therapy in order to defend himself or herself in any legal action initiated by the client.

- The client is less than 16 years old and the therapist has reason to believe that the child has been a victim of a crime such as child abuse. In fact, the psychologist is required to report to the police or to a child welfare agency within 36 hours any suspicion he or she has that the child client has been physically abused, including any suspicion of sexual molestation.

- The client initiated therapy in hopes of evading the law for having committed a crime or for planning to do so.

- The therapist judges that the client is a danger to self or to others and disclosure of information is necessary to ward off such danger (recall Focus on Discovery 18.2 on Tarasoff).

In Canada, as seen in the Supreme Court of Canada's decision in Smith v. Jones, even formally privileged solicitor-client relationships may be pierced where an individual is seen by a consulting mental health practitioner to constitute an imminent risk of serious bodily harm to an identifiable person or class of persons.

WHO IS THE CLIENT OR PATIENT?

Is it always clear to the clinician who the client is? In private therapy, when an adult pays a clinician a fee for help with a personal problem that has nothing to do with the legal system, the consulting individual is clearly the client. But an individual may be seen by a clinician for an evaluation of his or her competency to stand trial, or the clinician may be hired by an individual's family to assist in civil commitment proceedings. Perhaps the clinician is employed by a provincial psychiatric hospital as a regular staff member and sees a particular patient about problems in controlling aggressive impulses.

It should be clear, although it seldom is clear, that in these instances the clinician is serving more than one client. In addition to the patient, he or she serves the family or the province, and it is incumbent on the mental health professional to inform the patient that this is so. Verdun-Jones (2000) from Simon Fraser University has written extensively on the conflict faced by clinicians who must be true to their clinical role and protect the client's rights while at the same time ensuring that the rights of the general public are also protected. This dual allegiance does not necessarily indicate that the patient's own interests will be sacrificed, but it does mean that discussions will not inevitably remain secret and that the clinician may in the future act in a way that displeases the individual.

CHOICE OF GOALS

Ideally, the client sets the goals for therapy, but in practice, it is naive to assume that some goals are not imposed by the therapist and may even go against the wishes of the client. For example, a school system may want to institute a program that will teach children to "be still, be quiet, be docile" (Winett & Winkler, 1972, p. 499). Many behaviour therapists have assumed that young children should be compliant, not only because the teacher can then run a more orderly class, but because children are assumed to learn better when they are so. But do we really know that the most efficient and most enjoyable learning takes place when children are forced to remain quietly in their seats? Some advocates of open classrooms believe that curiosity and initiative, even in the youngest elementary school pupil, are at least as important as the acquisition of academic skills.

As is generally the case in psychology, evidence is less plentiful than strongly held and vehemently defended opinions. But it is clear that any professionals consulted by a school system have to be mindful of their own personal biases with respect to goals and should be prepared to work toward different ones if the parents and school personnel so wish. Any therapist has the option of not working for a client whose goals and proposed means of attaining them are abhorrent in his or her view.

This question of goals is particularly complex in family and couples therapy (Margolin, 1982). If several people are clients simultaneously—inevitable in family treatment—an intervention that benefits one or more individuals may well work to the disadvantage of one or more others. This can happen if one partner in couples therapy really wants to end the relationship, but the other sees the therapy as a way to save it. Because people often do not openly express their real concerns and wishes at the very beginning of therapy, the therapist can already be deeply enmeshed in their lives before learning that the two partners have conflicting goals. For this reason, among others, couples and family therapy is particularly challenging.

CHOICE OF TECHNIQUES

The end does not justify the means. This canon is said to be intrinsic to a free society. For years, questions concerning behavioural techniques have been debated among professionals and have been the subject of court rulings. Perhaps because the various insight therapies de-emphasize direct efforts to change behaviour, they have seldom been scrutinized in the way behaviour therapy has. The very concreteness, specificity, and directiveness of behavioural techniques have called attention to them, as has their alignment with experimental psychology. Some find it offensive to believe that our understanding of human beings could possibly be advanced by employing rats and pigeons as analogues to humans.

Particular concern has been expressed about the ethics of inflicting pain for purposes of therapy. For some people, the term "behaviour therapy" conjures up an image of the violent protagonist in Stanley Kubrick's classic film *A Clockwork Orange*, eyes propped open with a torturous apparatus, being made nauseous by a drug while scenes of violence flash on a screen. Aversion-therapy programs never reach this level of coercion and drama, but certainly any such procedure entails making the patient uncomfortable, sometimes extremely so. Making patients vomit or cringe with pain from electric shock applied to the extremities are two aversion techniques worthy of their name. Can there be any circumstances that justify therapists' inflicting pain on clients?

Before quickly exclaiming, "No!", consider the following report.

THE PATIENT was a nine-month-old baby who had already been hospitalized three times for treatment of vomiting and chronic rumination (regurgitating food and rechewing it in the mouth). A number of diagnostic tests, including an EEG, plus surgery to remove a cyst on the right kidney, had revealed no biological basis for the problems, and several treatments, including a special diet, had been attempted without success. When referred to Lang and Melamed (1969), two behaviour therapists, the child was in critical condition and was being fed by tubes leading from the nose directly into the stomach. The attending physician had stated that the infant's life was in imminent danger if the vomiting could not be halted.

Treatment consisted of delivering a series of one-second-long electric shocks to the infant's calf each time he showed signs of beginning to vomit. Sessions followed feeding and lasted under an hour. After just two sessions, shock was rarely required, for the infant learned quickly to stop vomiting in order to avoid the shock. By the sixth session, he was able to fall asleep after eating. Nurses reported that the in-session inhibition of vomiting generalized as the infant progressively reduced his vomiting during the rest of the day and night. About two weeks later, the mother began to assume some care of the hospitalized child, and shortly thereafter the patient was discharged with virtually complete elimination of the life-threatening pattern of behaviour. Throughout the three weeks of treatment and observation, the child gained weight steadily. One month after discharge, the child weighed 21 pounds and was rated as fully recovered by the attending physician. Five months later, he weighed 26 pounds and was regarded as completely normal, both physically and psychologically. (Lang & Melamed, 1969).

The use of aversion therapy has been subject to an understandably high degree of regulation. An additional reason for administrative and judicial concern is that aversion techniques smack more of research than of standard therapy. The more established a therapeutic procedure, whether medical or psychological, the less likely it is to attract the attention of the courts or other governmental agencies. Paul and Lentz (1977) had a few very assaultive patients. Their account of administrative problems demonstrates that patients might be subject to more extreme procedures because of restrictions placed on the use of new techniques.

> Some consideration was given to the contingent use of mild electric shock. . . . However, early in the explorations of the necessary safeguards and review procedures to be followed before evaluating such methods, the department

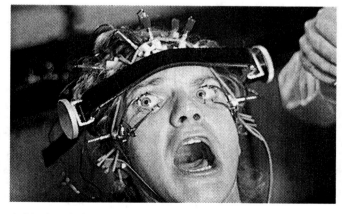

A Clockwork Orange depicted an extreme and fanciful example of aversion therapy.

director telephoned to explain that aversion conditioning was a politically sensitive issue. Therefore, more than the usual proposal, preparation, documentation, and committee reviews would be required—to the extent that approval would probably take about eighteen months. Instead, it was suggested that convulsive shock . . . be employed since "ECT is an accepted medical treatment." With those alternatives, our choice was to abandon either use of shock. (p. 499)

But should we be concerned only with physical pain? The anguish we suffer when a loved one dies is psychologically painful. It is perhaps more painful than an electric shock of 1,500 microamperes. Who is to say? Since we allow that pain can be psychological, should we forbid a Gestalt therapist from making a patient cry by confronting the patient with feelings that have been avoided for years? Should we forbid a psychoanalyst from guiding a patient to an insight that will likely cause great anguish, all the more so for the conflict's having been repressed for years?

THE RIGHT TO COMPETENT TREATMENT

Most readers of this text would assume that an important ethical principle that can almost go without saying is that people have a right to receive treatment from competent and highly trained individuals. Indeed, this provision is clearly stated in the ethical guidelines and standards of practice endorsed by the Canadian Psychological Association (2000). It is important to remain vigilant and ensure that the quality of care meets or exceeds expectations. This point is illustrated in Canadian Clinic Focus 18.1.

CANADIAN CLINIC FOCUS 18.1

ETHICAL CONCERNS AND THE MONTREUX CLINIC

The Montreux Clinic, an eating-disorder clinic in British Columbia run by Peggy Claude-Pierre, initially caused quite a sensation because eating disorders are notoriously difficult to treat. However, the Montreux Clinic appeared to have a very high success rate in curing the eating disorders of its clients. Claude-Pierre and her clinic received extensive coverage on a number of television shows, including ABC's *20/20*, *The Oprah Winfrey Show*, and, here in Canada, *The Pamela Wallin Show*. Claude-Pierre's approach received further attention when it was learned that Diana, Princess of Wales, had sought her advice for her bulimia problem.

Claude-Pierre's approach involved intensive treatment designed to restore the patient's sense of self-esteem in a safe and loving atmosphere. According to Claude-Pierre (1997), a vulnerability for eating disorders stems from "a confirmed negativity condition" that involves excessive self-criticism. A central goal of treatment was to reverse the negative mind through a variety of techniques and by treating the patient with unconditional love. Much of this treatment was based on insights that Claude-Pierre obtained as a result of her experiences as a mother of two daughters with eating disorders (see Claude-Pierre, 1997).

Unfortunately, problems eventually emerged at the Montreux Clinic. The clinic was investigated when a former employee made allegations to officials in the Victoria area that patients had been mistreated and that the staff were not trained adequately to address the problems of the eating-disorder patients. On December 1, 1999, the local medical officer, Dr. Richard Stanwick, ordered that the clinic be closed on January 31, 2000, because "the facility put the lives of its patients in danger with dishonesty and poor qualifications" (Sutherland, 1999, A23). Stanwick's report indicated that staff at the facility had physically restrained some patients and had forced others (including a 3-year-old boy who had been admitted even though the clinic's licence restricted it to patients 19 years or older) to eat. Also, few of the staff had university degrees and overall training was characterized as woefully inadequate. As director of the Montreux Clinic, Claude-Pierre did not have a graduate degree in psychology or a related discipline.

Initially, the Montreux Clinic appealed the order to close. However, the appeal was dropped and its operating licence was surrendered on August 25, 2000 (Meissner, 2000).

COMMENT

Unfortunately, it seems that the Montreux Clinic did indeed fail to meet a number of ethical standards prescribed by the Canadian Psychological Association (2000). One was an ethical principle described as the "Competence and Self-Knowledge" principle. The essence of this principle is that help providers must limit their assistance to those activities for which they have established their competence in carrying out to the benefit of others. Moreover, there should be no attempt to delegate activities to people who lack the competence to carry them out. This standard would have been violated if indeed it was the case that the staff lacked adequate training. A related principle that apparently was not met is one that involves maximizing the benefit to the patient; clinicians must provide the best possible service for those needing and seeking psychological services. This may include, but is not limited to, selecting interventions that are relevant to the needs and characteristics of the client and that have reasonable theoretical or empirically supported efficacy in light of those needs and characteristics. Another related concern with regard to the Montreux Clinic involved the general caring provisions set forth by the Canadian Psychological Association. If adequate treatment is not provided and coercive physical interventions are used, the best interests of the clients have not been served in terms of protecting and promoting their welfare.

THE ETHICAL AND LEGAL DIMENSIONS OF RECOVERED MEMORIES

In Chapter 7, we examined the scientific controversies raised by so-called recovered memories. The debate over the validity and reliability of reports of child abuse that surface when adults are in therapy created considerable ethical and legal concern (Ceci & Hembrooke, 1998). One of the most important of the guidelines issued by the American Psychiatric Association (1993) stipulates that therapists should remain neutral when a patient reports abuse. Because a given symptom—for example, avoidance of sexual contact—may have many possible origins, it is not ethical to attribute such symptoms to repressed memories of child sexual abuse (CSA) without corroborating evidence.

A problem with this laudable stance is the notion that therapists can maintain neutrality. Furthermore, some experts on sexual dysfunctions recommend that therapists inquire into possible sexual abuse whenever patients, especially women, report aversions to or disinterest in sex. The basic difficulty, then, is that many therapists are predisposed by their theorizing or by personal biases to believe that sexual abuse lies behind a wide range of psychological disorders. By the same token, therapists who do not believe that traumatic memories are often repressed may overlook CSA when it has taken place.

The statute of limitations has been extended in the United States, allowing those who believe they were abused as children to file suit 20 or more years after the abuse purportedly occurred. However, there was a backlash against these kinds of lawsuits, as accused parents and others (e.g., clergy, youth leaders, and other professionals in positions of trust with children and adolescents) denied such charges vigorously, and some patients recanted their allegations. This turn of events resulted in lawsuits being filed against therapists both by the accused parties and by the patients (MacNamara, 1993).

Probably the best-known legal incident concerned Gary Romona, whose daughter sued him for allegedly having molested her when she was a child. Romona, in turn, sued his daughter's therapist for having allegedly planted this erroneous idea into his daughter's mind. The father won a nearly half-million-dollar judgement (Kramer, 1995), at which point the daughter's suit against her father was dismissed. It is estimated that thousands of parents and other third parties filed or planned to file lawsuits against therapists (Lazo, 1995). In addition to a concern with possible therapist bias, these lawsuits are also concerned with particular treatments that may increase susceptibility to suggestion, such as hypnosis and sodium amytal (truth serum).

It is not clear, however, whether such lawsuits will be allowed to go forward in the future. In a case in California, a parent falsely accused of molesting a child on the basis of repressed memories elicited during therapy was not allowed to sue the therapist. The court ruled that a therapist must be free to act solely in the interests of the client and can be sued only by the client for negligent diagnosis or treatment. A therapist, the court said, is entitled to examine the possibility of past sexual abuse and should not be inhibited by the possibility of a suit by the alleged abuser. "The therapist risks utter professional failure in his or her duty to the patient if possible childhood sexual abuse is ignored," the judge said (Associated Press, February 18, 1999).

With the scientific status of the validity of recovered memories very much in dispute, legal scholars as well as professional associations advise extreme caution in dealing with the issue. The danger of false positives—concluding that there was abuse when there was not—is as serious a matter as the danger of false negatives—concluding that there was no abuse when there was.

CONCLUDING COMMENT

An underlying theme of this book concerns the nature of knowledge. How do we decide that we understand a phenomenon? The rules of science that govern our definition of and search for knowledge require theories that can be tested, studies that can be replicated, and data that are public. But given the complexity of abnormal behaviour and the vast areas of ignorance, far more extensive than the domains that have already been mapped by science as it is currently practised, we have great respect for theoreticians and clinicians, those inventive souls who make suppositions, offer hypotheses, follow hunches—all based on rather flimsy data, but holding some promise that scientific knowledge will be forthcoming.

This final chapter demonstrates again something emphasized at the very beginning of this book; namely, that the behavioural scientists and mental health professionals who conduct research and give treatment are only human beings. They suffer from the same foibles that sometimes plague non-specialists. They occasionally act with a certainty their evidence does not justify, and they sometimes fail to anticipate the moral and legal consequences of the ways in which they conduct research and apply the tentative findings of their young discipline. When society acts with great certainty on the basis of expert scientific opinion, particularly when that opinion denies to an individual the rights and respect accorded others, it may be good to let Szasz (1963) remind us that Sir Thomas Browne, a distinguished English physician, testified in an English court of law in 1664 that witches did indeed exist, "as everyone knew."

We hope that we have communicated in some measure our love for the subject matter and, more important, our commitment to the kind of questioning, doubting stance that wrests useful knowledge from nature and will yield more as new generations of scholars build on the achievements of their predecessors.

SUMMARY

- There are many legal and ethical issues related to treatment and research in psychopathology and intervention. Some civil liberties are rather routinely set aside when mental health professionals and the courts judge that mental illness has played a decisive role in determining an individual's behaviour.

- Criminal commitment sends a person to a hospital either before a trial for an alleged crime, because the person is deemed incompetent to stand trial, or after an acquittal by reason of not being criminally responsible on account of mental disorder.

- Several landmark cases in Canada and principles in Anglo-American law inform current thinking about the conditions under which a person who has committed a crime might be excused from legal responsibility for it. These decisions involve the notion that some people may not be able to distinguish between right and wrong (the M'Naghten Rules).

- There is an important difference between mental illness and insanity. The latter is a legal concept. A person can be diagnosed as mentally ill and yet be deemed sane enough both to stand trial and to be found guilty of a crime.

- A person who is considered mentally ill and dangerous to his- or herself and to others, though he or she has not broken a law, can be civilly committed to an institution or be allowed to live outside of a hospital, although sometimes only under supervision and with restrictions placed on his or her activities.

- There are a number of ethical issues concerning therapy and research: ethical restraints on what kinds of research are allowable, the duty of scientists to obtain informed consent from prospective human subjects, the right of clients to confidentiality, the setting of therapy goals, the choice of techniques, and memories of sexual abuse in childhood recovered during psychotherapy when the person is an adult.

KEY TERMS

civil commitment (p. 601)
confidentiality (p. 628)
community commitment (p. 609)
criminal commitment (p. 601)

informed consent (p. 627)
insanity defence (p. 602)
M'Naghten Rules (p. 603)
not criminally responsible (p. 602)

prior capable wish (p. 619)
privileged communication (p. 616)

REFLECTIONS: PAST, PRESENT, AND FUTURE

- Revisit the quote by Abram Hoffer at the beginning of this chapter. One strict interpretation is that people with serious and chronic mental disorders can't be rehabilitated while living in the community ("whose healing qualities clearly were not sufficient to prevent them from becoming sick in the first place") or staying with their families ("too sick, or too tired, or simply do not have the resources or the energy to cope with very sick patients"). What does Hoffer really mean? What is the implication of his statements? How do they tie in to the implications of our discussions about the problems with deinstitutionalization?

- We reviewed recommended changes to the mental health "system" and the treatment of people with chronic mental health problems. What changes do you think will occur in the next 25 years? What reforms will be implemented? Will there be discoveries of new drugs that will act as "magic

bullets" in the fight against disorders such as schizophrenia and bipolar disorder? Will there be breakthroughs in psychotherapy? What will it be like for the mentally ill in the next millennium? Will mental illness be all but eradicated, just as some illnesses such as leprosy or polio have been eliminated, at least in the Western world?

- Do you think that we will ever get rid of the stigma associated with mental illness? Do you think that the goal of integrating people with serious and chronic mental health problems will ever become "reality rather than rhetoric" (Goering, 2000, p. 356)? Do you think that scarce dollars in the mental health area will be allocated to other priorities in health care as a consequence of the "baby boomer" generation developing physical health problems that put pressure on the health care system in Canada?